Azure for Decision Mal

The essential guide to Azure for business leaders

Jack Lee

Jason Milgram

David Rendón

BIRMINGHAM—MUMBAI

Azure for Decision Makers

First Edition

Copyright © 2023 Packt Publishing

Acquisition Editor: Mamta Yadav

Lead Development Editor: Alex Patterson

Development Editor: Siddhant Jain

Content Development Editor: Afzal Shaikh

Project Coordinator: Yash Basil

Copy Editor: Safis Editing

Proofreader: Safis Editing

Production Designer: Deepak Chavan

Production reference: 1060923

Published by Packt Publishing Ltd.

Grosvenor House, 11 St Paul's Square, Birmingham, B3 1RB, UK.

ISBN 978-1-83763-991-5

www.packtpub.com

Contributors

About the authors

Jack Lee is a Microsoft MVP and an Azure Certified Solutions Architect with a passion for software development, cloud, and DevOps innovations. He is an active Microsoft tech community contributor and has presented at various user groups and conferences, among them the Global Azure Bootcamp at Microsoft Canada. Jack is an experienced mentor and judge at hackathons and is also the president of a user group that focuses on Azure, DevOps, and software development. He has authored numerous books published by Packt, notably *Azure for Architects*, *Azure Strategy* and *Implementation Guide*, and *Cloud Analytics with Microsoft Azure*. In addition, he has earned multiple certifications including Microsoft Azure Solutions Architect Expert and Microsoft DevOps Engineer Expert. You can follow Jack on Twitter at `jlee_consulting`.

Jason Milgram is an SVP and Azure leader at OZ Digital, headquartered in Fort Lauderdale, FL. Jason has been working with computers ever since he bought his first, a Timex/Sinclair 1000, in 6th grade and taught himself BASIC programming. Prior to OZ, Jason was CTO of financial services at Hitachi Solutions in Irvine, CA, chief architect at i3 in Fairfax, VA, chief architect at SAIC in Reston, VA, 1st VP cloud solutions architect at City National Bank of Florida in Miami, FL, and VP of platform architecture and engineering at Champion Solutions Group in Boca Raton, FL. Earlier in his career, he worked in IT for clients such as IBM, the US Department of Justice, Florida Power and Light, Chase Manhattan Bank, PricewaterhouseCoopers, Kodak, and Iris Associates (creator of Lotus Notes). He was also a sergeant in the US Army Reserve, serving from 1990 to 1998. Jason was educated at the University of Cincinnati and the Massachusetts Institute of Technology – Sloan School of Management. As a public speaker, Jason has given over 100 presentations at conferences and user groups on cloud computing, Microsoft Azure, Enterprise Mobility + Security, and launching a tech start-up. He is a Microsoft Azure MVP (2010-present), a young adult author, and a cellist.

Dave Rendón, Microsoft MVP and Microsoft Certified Trainer, is a highly regarded expert in the Azure cloud platform. With over 15 years of experience as an IT professional, he has been deeply committed to Microsoft technologies, especially Azure, since 2010. With a proven track record of leading and driving strategic success, David has over seven years of management experience and technical leadership and collaboration skills. David delivers private technical training classes worldwide, covering EMEA, South America, and the US, and is a frequent speaker at renowned IT events such as Microsoft Ignite, Global Azure, and local user group gatherings in the US, Europe, and Latin America. Stay connected with David on LinkedIn at `/daverndn`.

About the reviewers

Kapil Bansal is a PhD scholar and lead DevOps engineer at S&P Global Market Intelligence, India. He has more than 15 years of experience in the IT industry, having worked on Azure cloud computing (PaaS, IaaS, and SaaS), Azure Stack, DevSecOps, Kubernetes, Terraform, Office 365, SharePoint, release management, **application lifecycle management (ALM)**, **Information Technology Infrastructure Library (ITIL)**, and Six Sigma. He has completed a certification program in *Advanced Programme in Strategy for Leaders* from IIM Lucknow and *Advanced Programme in Cyber Security and Cyber Defense* from IIT Kanpur.

He has worked with companies such as IBM India Pvt Ltd, HCL Technologies, NIIT Technologies, Encore Capital Group, and Xavient Software Solutions, Noida, and has served multiple clients based in the US, the UK, and Africa, such as T-Mobile, World Bank Group, H&M, WBMI, Encore Capital, and Bharti Airtel (India and Africa).

Kapil also reviewed *Hands-On Kubernetes on Azure* and *Azure Networking Cookbook*, published by Packt Publishing, as well as *Practical Microsoft Azure IaaS* and *Beginning SharePoint Communication Sites*, published by Apress, and many more.

Aaditya Maruthi Pokkunuri is an experienced senior cloud database engineer with over 13 years of experience working in the information technology and services industry. He is skilled in performance tuning, MS SQL database server administration, SSIS, SSRS, Power BI, and SQL development.

He possesses strong knowledge of replication, clustering, SQL Server high-availability options, and ITIL processes. His expertise lies in Windows administration tasks, Active Directory, and Microsoft Azure technologies. He also possesses strong knowledge of MySQL, MariaDB, and MySQL Aurora database engines. He has expertise in the AWS cloud area and is an AWS Solutions Architect Associate with the AWS Database Specialty.

Aaditya is a strong information technology professional with a bachelor's degree in computer science and engineering from Sastra University, Tamil Nadu.

Table of Contents

5

Automation and Governance in Azure   101

6

Preface

Azure for Decision Makers covers why and how an organization can achieve a successful migration to the cloud. This book discusses different kinds of cloud solutions and describes how to make the best decisions when modernizing your organization by migrating to the cloud. *Azure for Decision Makers* ensures that you can make the most of the cost optimization, efficiency, automation, and security that a cloud solution with Microsoft Azure provides.

Who this book is for

This book is for business decision makers and IT decision makers who are considering a migration to the cloud as part of their organization's modernization strategy.

What this book covers

Chapter 1, Introduction, covers the reasons an organization might engage with cloud computing, and why Microsoft Azure in particular is a compelling choice. It goes on to discuss the various types of cloud environments and crucial security and governance considerations when migrating to the cloud.

Chapter 2, Modernizing with Hybrid, Multicloud, and Edge Computing, covers how these modernizing approaches can drive significant efficiency, agility, and innovation improvements for any organization. It also covers the set of tools Microsoft Azure provides for a modern, flexible, and secure infrastructure transition.

Chapter 3, Migration and Modernization, describes how the benefits of the cloud can help businesses stay ahead of the curve and drive innovation in their industry, as well as how an organization can accelerate its cloud adoption journey.

Chapter 4, Maximizing Azure Security Benefits for Your Organization, covers best practices for securing workloads on Microsoft Azure, Microsoft Sentinel as a tool for intelligent security analytics, and Microsoft Defender for Cloud, Identity, Endpoint, and Cloud Apps, each of which can help identify suspicious activity and prevent advanced attacks.

Chapter 5, Automation and Governance in Azure, explains the importance of automation and governance, discussing the two native Microsoft **Infrastructure as Code (IaC)** frameworks: **Azure Resource Manager (ARM)** templates and Bicep. Governance is a critical aspect of managing resources on Azure, and the tools and services available to facilitate this are also covered.

Chapter 6, Maximizing Efficiency and Cost Savings in Azure, discusses the impact of cost optimization in the cloud, and its place as one of the five pillars of the Microsoft Azure Well-Architected Framework.

It goes on to explain the different ways that Azure Advisor can help organizations optimize Azure resources based on usage patterns, as part of a comprehensive cost optimization strategy.

Chapter 7, Next Steps, summarizes the book and delivers guidance for further action.

To get the most out of this book

You do not require any existing knowledge of Azure or cloud computing.

Get in touch

Feedback from our readers is always welcome.

General feedback: If you have questions about any aspect of this book, email us at customercare@packtpub.com and mention the book title in the subject of your message.

Errata: Although we have taken every care to ensure the accuracy of our content, mistakes do happen. If you find a mistake in this book, we would be grateful to you for sending the report to us. Please visit www.packtpub.com/support/errata and fill in the form.

Piracy: If you come across any illegal copies of our works in any form on the internet, we would be grateful to you for providing us with the location address or website name. Please contact us at copyright@packt.com with a link to the material.

Becoming an author: If there is a topic that you have expertise in and you are interested in either writing or contributing to a book, please visit authors.packtpub.com.

Download a free PDF copy of this book

Thanks for purchasing this book!

Do you like to read on the go but are unable to carry your print books everywhere?

Is your eBook purchase not compatible with the device of your choice?

Don't worry, now with every Packt book you get a DRM-free PDF version of that book at no cost.

Read anywhere, any place, on any device. Search, copy, and paste code from your favorite technical books directly into your application.

The perks don't stop there, you can get exclusive access to discounts, newsletters, and great free content in your inbox daily

Follow these simple steps to get the benefits:

1. Scan the QR code or visit the link below

https://packt.link/free-ebook/9781837639915

2. Submit your proof of purchase

3. That's it! We'll send your free PDF and other benefits to your email directly

1
Introduction

Over the years, cloud computing has seen significant adoption among organizations, Fortune 500 companies, and governments alike. This widespread adoption is due to the multiple benefits of cloud technology, such as cost savings, increased agility, and enhanced scalability.

The rise of cloud adoption can be attributed to the realization that cloud computing provides unparalleled flexibility, scalability, and cost-effectiveness. As a result, organizations of all sizes have quickly embraced cloud services to drive digital transformation and stay ahead in the competitive market. A recent article from BBC Future indicates that over 90% of enterprises have adopted some form of cloud computing, with most choosing a hybrid or multicloud strategy.

More than 95% of Fortune 500 companies trust and run their business on Azure today, and many of them take advantage of Azure's hybrid capabilities to fuel innovation and deliver great business outcomes.[1] This shift has enabled Fortune 500 companies to innovate faster, minimize downtime, and reduce operational costs while staying ahead in a rapidly evolving digital landscape.

Around the world, governments and a range of industries, such as healthcare, finance, retail, and manufacturing, have turned to cloud computing to revitalize their IT systems, fortify data security, and boost the quality of the services they deliver. With the promotion of strategies such as cloud-first or cloud-smart, they have successfully improved their operational efficiencies, smoothened their workflow processes, and complied with strict data protection laws. Moreover, these sectors have harnessed the power of cloud technology to elevate their operations, enrich their customer experiences, foster innovation, and formulate new business models and data-driven insights. The quick and widespread adoption of cloud computing underscores its critical role in revolutionizing how we utilize computational power and manage data, demonstrating its exponential growth over recent decades.

In this chapter, we will cover the following topics:

- Cloud computing models
- The shared responsibility model from Microsoft
- Benefits of adopting Azure
- How to get started with Azure

---

1 https://tinyurl.com/bdfct99e

Evolution of Microsoft Azure

In the ever-evolving realm of cloud computing, Microsoft Azure has persistently pioneered groundbreaking initiatives and accomplished significant milestones. Understanding these pivotal moments offers an enriching perspective on Azure's journey and growth and provides invaluable insights for business decision-makers. By recognizing Azure's key achievements and understanding their implications, we can better navigate the strategic landscape of cloud computing, anticipate future trends, and use these insights for effective decision-making. The following list enumerates some of these notable milestones and offers a brief description of each.

Important Microsoft Azure milestones with brief descriptions:

- 2008 – Project "Red Dog": Microsoft started developing its cloud computing platform, initially known as Project "Red Dog," led by Dave Cutler and Amitabh Srivastava

- 2010 – Windows Azure launch: Microsoft officially launched Windows Azure, marking its entry into the cloud computing space as a PaaS service

- 2012 – IaaS support: Microsoft expanded Azure to support IaaS, enabling customers to deploy and manage virtual machines and other infrastructure components

- 2014 – Rebranding to Microsoft Azure: Windows Azure was rebranded as Microsoft Azure, reflecting the platform's support for multiple operating systems, programming languages, and services

- 2014 – Azure Machine Learning: Microsoft introduced Azure Machine Learning, a cloud-based service for building, deploying, and managing machine learning models

- 2015 – Azure IoT Suite: Microsoft released the Azure IoT Suite, providing a set of preconfigured solutions and services for Internet of Things applications

- 2016 – Azure Functions: Microsoft launched Azure Functions, a serverless compute service allowing developers to run event-driven code without managing infrastructure

- 2016 – Azure N-series virtual machines: Microsoft announced the general availability of Azure N-Series virtual machines, powered by NVIDIA GPUs, designed for high-performance computing and AI workloads

- 2016 – OpenAI and Microsoft begin their partnership: OpenAI agreed to use Microsoft's Azure cloud-computing software to run its AI experiments

- 2016 – Azure Data Lake released

- 2018 – Azure Data Box Edge: Microsoft announced the general availability of Azure Data Box Edge, a hardware appliance for data processing and transfer to Azure, enabling edge computing

- 2018 – Azure Databricks released

- 2019 – Azure Kubernetes Service: Microsoft made **Azure Kubernetes Service (AKS)** generally available, offering a managed Kubernetes service for easy container orchestration

- 2019 – Azure Arc: Microsoft unveiled Azure Arc, allowing customers to extend Azure management and services to hybrid environments and other cloud platforms

- 2019 – Microsoft invested $1 billion in OpenAI to jointly develop new supercomputing tech, building on their 2016 partnership

- 2020 – Azure Synapse Analytics: Microsoft announced the general availability of Azure Synapse Analytics, an integrated analytics service that combines big data and data warehousing

- 2020 – Azure Communication Services: Microsoft introduced Azure Communication Services, a fully managed communication platform for integrating voice, video, chat, and SMS into applications

- 2020 – Azure Kinect DK released: A developer kit with advanced AI sensors for building sophisticated computer vision and speech models

- 2021 – Azure Marketplace: By mid-2021, there were over 16,000 products and services offered on the Microsoft Azure Marketplace

- 2021 – Azure Virtual Desktop and Windows 365: Introduced the capability to deliver a secure hybrid workplace with Azure Virtual Desktop and Windows 365

- 2021 – Azure Purview: The cloud-native data governance solution Azure Purview was released

- 2021 – Azure Communication Services released: This is a fully managed communication platform that enables you to securely build communication features and connected user experiences across applications running on any device

- 2021 – Azure Quantum: This is a cloud service that offers access to a variety of quantum computing and optimization solutions

- 2022 – Azure Space became generally available: Extend Azure capabilities anywhere in the world with Space infrastructure

- 2022 – Azure Spatial Anchors released: This is a cross-platform developer service that allows you to create **mixed reality** (**MR**) experiences using objects that persist in their location across devices over time

- 2022 – Microsoft 365 Copilot Preview announced

- 2023 – OpenAI investment: Microsoft announced a new multi-year $10 billion investment in OpenAI

- 2023 – Azure OpenAI: Release of Azure OpenAI Service

- 2023 – Microsoft Security Copilot Preview: This provides generative AI insights for faster incident response

- 2023 – Azure Storage Mover: This is a fully managed migration service that enables you to migrate your files and folders to Azure Storage

As we look back at these milestones, it is clear that Microsoft Azure's journey is marked by a consistent pursuit of innovation, advancement, and service enhancement. Each milestone has played a critical role in shaping Azure into the robust, reliable, and highly adaptable cloud computing platform it is today. In addition, these milestones provide crucial insights into Azure's capabilities for business decision-makers, offering a foundation for making informed strategic choices in a dynamic technological environment. As Azure continues to evolve and redefine the boundaries of cloud computing, we can anticipate even more transformative developments on the horizon.

IaaS, PaaS, and SaaS

In today's rapidly evolving digital landscape, businesses must adopt and adapt to new technologies to stay competitive and meet the needs of their customers. As a result, cloud computing has emerged as a critical enabler of business success, offering a wide range of solutions that help organizations streamline their operations, reduce costs, and drive innovation. One key aspect of cloud computing is the variety of service models it encompasses—**infrastructure as a service (IaaS)**, **platform as a service (PaaS)**, and **software as a service (SaaS)**. This section will highlight these three service models, delving into their unique benefits and use cases and helping business decision-makers understand how each model can contribute to their organization's growth and digital transformation journey.

IaaS

IaaS provides virtualized computing resources over the internet. It allows businesses to rent essential IT infrastructure components, such as storage, networking, and computing power, on a pay-as-you-go basis, eliminating the need for physical hardware and maintenance.

Cost efficiency	Pay only for the resources you use, avoiding upfront investments in hardware and maintenance.
Scalability	Quickly scale resources up or down according to your business needs.
Flexibility	Choose from various hardware and software configurations to meet specific requirements.
Reduced maintenance burden	Offload the responsibility of managing and maintaining physical infrastructure to the cloud provider.
Increased performance	Access scalable computing resources on demand, ensuring optimal performance levels.
Security	Receive robust infrastructure with built-in security measures, reducing the burden of managing and maintaining your physical servers.

PaaS

PaaS offers a platform that enables developers to build, deploy, and manage applications without worrying about the underlying infrastructure. It provides the tools, frameworks, and services for application development, streamlining the process and reducing the time to market.

Faster development and deployment	Access to pre-built tools and frameworks simplifies the application development process.
Scalability	PaaS platforms automatically scale resources to accommodate changing application demands.
Reduced complexity	Developers can focus on writing code and features without worrying about infrastructure management.
Enhanced collaboration	Teams can efficiently work together on projects, regardless of their physical location.
Enhanced security	Expect built-in data protection and regular security updates, safeguarding your sensitive information and applications.

SaaS

SaaS delivers software applications over the internet on a subscription basis. Users can access the software and its features through a web browser without installing or maintaining the application on their devices.

Accessibility	Accessing applications from any device with an internet connection allows remote work and collaboration.
Cost savings	Eliminate upfront software licensing costs and ongoing maintenance expenses.
Automatic updates	SaaS providers manage updates and security patches, ensuring users have the latest software version.
Customization	Many SaaS applications offer customizable features to suit specific business requirements.
Scalability	Effortlessly adjust the number of users and service levels needed according to needs.
Integration	Expect seamless integration with existing systems and third-party applications.

IaaS, PaaS, and SaaS offer different levels of cloud services, each catering to specific needs and requirements. By understanding these models and their benefits, you can make informed decisions on which cloud services best fit your organization's needs.

Public, private, hybrid, multicloud, and edge

As digital transformation continues to revolutionize how organizations operate, business decision-makers face an ever-expanding array of cloud computing options. Each model offers unique benefits and challenges, making it essential for decision-makers to understand the nuances of public, private, hybrid, multicloud, and edge computing environments. This section aims to briefly guide you through the complexities of these cloud computing models, helping you make informed choices that align with your organization's strategic goals and requirements.

By understanding these computing environments, you will be better equipped to evaluate which approach best suits your organization's unique circumstances and objectives. The following table highlights critical factors to consider when planning your cloud adoption journey, ensuring a seamless transition that delivers maximum value and supports sustainable growth.

Public cloud

Public cloud refers to a computing environment where cloud service providers offer computing resources, such as storage, networking, and processing power, over the internet on a shared infrastructure. Businesses can access these resources on a pay-as-you-go basis, allowing them to scale their IT needs efficiently without investing in and maintaining physical hardware.

Cost-effective	The pay-as-you-go pricing model reduces upfront costs and ongoing maintenance expenses.
Scalability	Quickly scale resources up or down to match demand.
Flexibility	Access a wide variety of services and features.
Simplified management	The cloud provider handles infrastructure maintenance and updates.
Global reach	Utilize datacenters and services available worldwide.

Private cloud

A private cloud is a computing environment where a single organization exclusively uses dedicated resources, either on-premises or hosted by a third-party provider. Private clouds offer more control, customization, and security than public clouds, making them suitable for organizations with strict data privacy and compliance requirements.

Enhanced security	Greater control over data and network security measures.
Customization	Tailor the infrastructure and services to meet specific organizational needs.
Compliance	Facilitate adherence to industry-specific regulations and standards.
Dedicated resources	Enjoy the consistent performance and dedicated hardware.
Control	Retain more significant control over the cloud environment and underlying infrastructure.

Hybrid cloud

A hybrid cloud combines public and private cloud elements, allowing organizations to utilize the best of both worlds. By making use of a hybrid cloud, businesses can take advantage of the cost-efficiency and scalability of public cloud services for less-sensitive workloads while maintaining sensitive data and critical applications on a private cloud for enhanced security and control.

Best of both worlds	Combine the benefits of public and private cloud environments.
Flexibility	Move workloads between public and private clouds based on needs and requirements.
Optimized cost	Allocate resources across public and private clouds to optimize costs.
Enhanced security	Keep sensitive data on-premises while making use of public cloud resources for non-sensitive workloads.
Business continuity	Improve disaster recovery and backup strategies by distributing data and applications across multiple environments.

Multicloud

Multicloud strategically uses multiple cloud service providers for different tasks or workloads. Organizations adopt multicloud strategies to avoid vendor lock-in, enhance performance by utilizing the strengths of various providers, and increase redundancy to mitigate risks associated with relying on a single provider.

Avoid vendor lock-in	Distribute workloads across multiple cloud providers to minimize dependence on a single provider.
Flexibility	Choose the best services and features from each cloud provider to suit specific needs.
Enhanced resilience	Improve reliability by distributing resources across multiple cloud providers.
Cost optimization	Make use of the pricing and service advantages of different providers.
Innovation	Access the latest features and technologies from multiple providers.

Edge computing

Edge computing is a distributed computing paradigm that brings data processing and storage closer to the source of data, such as IoT devices or sensors, reducing latency and bandwidth consumption. By processing data at the edge of the network, businesses can enable real-time analytics, improve the user experience, and increase the efficiency of their operations.

Reduced latency	Process data closer to the source, minimizing data processing and transmission delays.
Improved performance	Offload processing tasks to edge devices, reducing the burden on central servers.
Enhanced security	Limit the exposure of sensitive data by processing it locally.
Scalability	Deploy edge computing resources as needed to support growing workloads.
Real-time analytics	Enable faster decision-making and insights by processing data at the edge.

Understanding these cloud deployment models will help you decide on the most suitable cloud strategy for your organization. Each model has unique advantages, and the right choice depends on your business requirements, budget, and compliance needs.

Importance of the shared responsibility model

As we have explored the various cloud service models, including IaaS, PaaS, and SaaS, and the different types of cloud environments, such as public, private, hybrid, multicloud, and edge computing, it becomes evident that each solution offers unique benefits to businesses. However, the advantages of these models can only be fully realized if organizations clearly understand their responsibilities in maintaining security and compliance. This brings us to the crucial concept of the shared responsibility model. The following section will briefly cover the importance of understanding and implementing the shared responsibility model, ensuring that the cloud service provider and the customer work together to create a secure and compliant environment. This collaboration is essential for protecting sensitive data, minimizing risks, and ultimately enabling your organization to harness the full potential of cloud technology.

The shared responsibility model outlines the division of responsibilities between cloud service providers and their customers regarding security, compliance, and overall management. Understanding this division is crucial for ensuring your organization's data and applications are protected in the cloud.

In the shared responsibility model, the cloud service provider is responsible for securing the underlying infrastructure, which includes physical hardware, datacenters, and the network. On the other hand, the customer is responsible for securing the data, applications, and configurations within the cloud environment.

The exact division of responsibilities can vary depending on the cloud service model being used. Here's a brief overview:

- **IaaS**: In IaaS, the cloud provider is responsible for securing the infrastructure components, such as virtual machines, storage, and networking. On the other hand, the customer is responsible for securing the operating systems, applications, data, and network configurations within the virtual machines.

- **PaaS**: In PaaS, the cloud provider secures the infrastructure and the underlying platform, including the operating system, middleware, and runtime environment. The customer is responsible for securing the applications and data they deploy within the platform.

- **SaaS**: In SaaS, the cloud provider takes on the most responsibility, securing the infrastructure, platform, and application layers. Customers are mainly responsible for securing their data and access management, such as user permissions and authentication.

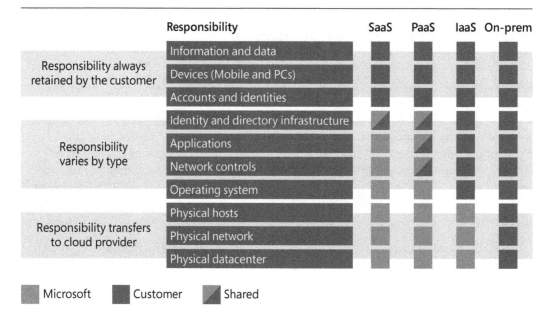

Figure 1.1: Areas of responsibility between customer and Microsoft

Understanding the shared responsibility model helps ensure that your organization takes the necessary steps to secure its data and applications in the cloud. Therefore, it is crucial to clearly understand your responsibilities and implement proper security measures to complement the protection provided by the cloud service provider.

The shared responsibility model is a fundamental concept in cloud computing that defines the security and management tasks division between cloud providers and their customers. By understanding and adhering to this model, your organization can effectively mitigate risks and maintain a secure cloud environment.

Reasons for adopting Azure

Adopting Microsoft Azure can provide organizations with a comprehensive and secure cloud platform that enables scalability, cost savings, and flexibility. Azure's extensive range of services, including IaaS, PaaS, and SaaS, caters to various business needs and supports digital transformation. Microsoft's focus on enterprise customers, hybrid, multicloud, and edge computing capabilities, and seamless integration with existing Microsoft products make Azure an attractive choice for organizations already invested in the Microsoft ecosystem. Additionally, Azure's commitment to advanced technologies, such as AI, machine learning, and large-scale data analytics, ensures that organizations can stay at the forefront of innovation.

High availability and scalability

High availability and scalability are critical factors for businesses looking to harness the power of cloud computing to drive innovation and growth. With Azure's robust infrastructure, extensive global network, and advanced technologies, organizations can seamlessly meet their ever-evolving needs and demands without compromising reliability or performance. In addition, business decision-makers can gain insights into how Azure's flexibility and resilience can empower their organizations to respond effectively to changing market conditions, accommodate growth, and maintain uninterrupted operations in today's highly competitive landscape.

Let's explore the key reasons business decision-makers should adopt Azure for its high availability and scalability capabilities:

- **Built-in redundancy**: Azure offers built-in redundancy across its infrastructure, with multiple regional datacenters. This ensures that if one datacenter experiences an issue, other datacenters within the same region can automatically pick up the workload, minimizing downtime and maintaining business continuity.

- **Scalable infrastructure**: Azure's scalable infrastructure allows organizations to quickly adjust resources to accommodate changing workloads, ensuring optimal performance and cost efficiency. Whether scaling up during peak demand or down during quieter periods, Azure provides the flexibility to adapt to business needs.

- **Autoscaling capabilities**: Azure offers autoscaling capabilities that automatically adjust resources based on real-time demand, ensuring consistent performance and reducing the risk of overprovisioning or underprovisioning. This feature helps maintain application performance but also helps control costs by only using the resources needed.

- **Fault tolerance**: Azure's fault-tolerant infrastructure is designed to withstand failures at the hardware, software, and network levels, ensuring the continuous operation of critical applications and services. This resilience is crucial for organizations that depend on always-on availability for business success.

- **Load balancing**: Azure provides load-balancing capabilities that evenly distribute traffic across multiple instances of an application or service, preventing bottlenecks and improving overall performance. This ensures a smooth user experience and supports the efficient operation of applications with varying workloads.

- **Disaster recovery**: Azure offers comprehensive disaster recovery solutions that protect organizations from data loss and minimize downtime during a disaster. These solutions include geo-redundant storage, backup services, and site recovery, providing peace of mind for business decision-makers.

Adopting Azure for its high availability and scalability capabilities enables organizations to deliver consistent performance, maintain business continuity, and support growth without compromising reliability. Business decision-makers should carefully consider these benefits as they evaluate their cloud adoption strategy and work toward achieving their strategic objectives.

Reliability and predictability

Reliability and predictability are crucial factors for organizations looking to adopt cloud services. As a leading cloud service provider, Microsoft Azure ensures that its platform offers the highest levels of reliability and predictability for businesses.

Microsoft Azure provides comprehensive reliability features such as **Service-Level Agreements (SLAs)** for guaranteed uptime, robust backup and disaster recovery solutions, and proactive monitoring to ensure the optimal performance and availability of applications and services:

- **SLAs**: Microsoft Azure is committed to delivering consistent, high-quality performance across its services. To this end, Azure provides comprehensive SLAs that outline the performance and uptime guarantees for its various offerings. These SLAs offer businesses the assurance they need when choosing Azure as their cloud platform, as they can be confident that their mission-critical applications and services will remain operational and available.

- **Backup and disaster recovery**: Azure ensures the reliability of its services by offering robust backup and disaster recovery options for organizations. Using Azure's geo-redundant storage and globally distributed datacenters, businesses can create a resilient infrastructure that safeguards their data and applications from potential disruptions, such as hardware failures or natural disasters. This, in turn, minimizes downtime and ensures the continuity of operations.

- **Proactive monitoring**: Azure provides a suite of monitoring and diagnostics tools that enable businesses to proactively identify and address potential issues, ensuring the reliability and stability of their cloud infrastructure. Tools such as Azure Monitor and Application Insights offer real-time insights into the health and performance of applications and services, enabling organizations to make informed decisions and optimize their cloud resources for maximum reliability.

Microsoft Azure also offers predictability features that include cost management and optimization for budget control, performance and latency improvements for consistent user experience, and a consistent management experience for streamlined operations across the cloud environment:

- **Cost management and optimization**: Predictability in terms of cost is a crucial concern for businesses adopting cloud services. Azure addresses this by offering a range of cost management and optimization tools, such as Azure Cost Management and Azure Advisor. These tools give businesses visibility into their cloud spending patterns, helping them identify potential savings and optimize their cloud resources to achieve the best performance at the lowest possible cost.

- **Performance and latency**: Azure is designed to deliver consistent, high-performance experiences for users across the globe. With its extensive network of datacenters and a global content delivery network, Azure ensures low latency and high-speed connectivity for businesses' applications and services. This enables organizations to provide a responsive and reliable experience for their end-users, regardless of location.

- **Consistent management experience**: Consistent management experience is an essential aspect of predictability in Azure, as it enables business decision-makers to streamline their organization's cloud operations with ease and efficiency. Azure provides a unified management interface through the Azure portal, Azure PowerShell, and the Azure CLI, allowing businesses to seamlessly manage and monitor all their cloud resources, applications, and services across various platforms and environments. This consistent management experience simplifies deploying, configuring, and maintaining cloud infrastructure and ensures that organizations can easily predict and plan their cloud operations. As a result, businesses can focus on innovation and growth while enjoying the benefits of a predictable and dependable cloud platform in Azure.

Microsoft Azure's focus on reliability and predictability makes it a compelling choice for business decision-makers seeking a dependable cloud platform. With robust SLAs, backup and disaster recovery options, proactive monitoring and diagnostics, cost management tools, and high-performance infrastructure, Azure offers organizations the confidence and predictability they need to succeed in a rapidly evolving digital landscape.

Hybrid flexibility

In today's dynamic business environment, organizations need the flexibility to adapt to changing requirements and seamlessly integrate various IT resources. Hybrid flexibility in Microsoft Azure offers a powerful solution to bridge the gap between on-premises infrastructure, the public cloud, and edge computing. Azure's hybrid solutions empower businesses to optimize their IT investments, streamline processes, and achieve greater agility. Azure's comprehensive suite of hybrid services and tools enables organizations to harness the best of both worlds, providing a robust, secure, and scalable foundation for innovation and growth in the digital era.

This section will briefly explore why business decision-makers should adopt Azure for hybrid flexibility.

- **Seamless integration**: Azure's hybrid solutions are designed to work seamlessly with your existing infrastructure, reducing the complexity and cost of integration. This enables organizations to make use of the investments they have already made in on-premises hardware and software while tapping into the benefits of the cloud.

- **Consistent management experience**: Azure provides a consistent management experience across on-premises, public cloud, and edge environments, enabling IT teams to simplify administration, reduce overhead, and increase efficiency. Organizations can streamline their operations and minimize the learning curve using familiar tools and processes.

- **Improved security and compliance**: With Azure's hybrid offerings, organizations can maintain the necessary security and compliance controls for sensitive workloads while benefiting from Azure's advanced security features. This provides a balanced approach to ensuring data protection and regulatory compliance across different environments.

- **Greater flexibility and agility**: Hybrid flexibility in Azure allows organizations to choose the best deployment model for their applications and workloads, whether on-premises, in the public cloud, or at the edge. This enables businesses to respond to changing market conditions and customer needs more effectively, driving innovation and competitive advantage.

- **Cost optimization**: By adopting a hybrid approach with Azure, organizations can optimize their IT costs using the most suitable infrastructure for their workloads. This means taking advantage of cost-effective cloud resources when needed while maintaining on-premises investments for specific use cases.

- **Enhanced application performance**: Azure's hybrid solutions enable organizations to place workloads closer to end-users or data sources, improving performance and reducing latency. This ensures a better user experience and supports data-intensive applications that require real-time processing and analytics.

Microsoft Azure's hybrid flexibility features empower organizations to harness their IT resources' full potential while driving innovation, efficiency, and growth. Business decision-makers should carefully consider the benefits of hybrid flexibility in Azure as they navigate the complexities of today's digital landscape and strive to create value for their stakeholders.

Innovation

Microsoft's commitment to innovation is evident in its continuous development and investment in cutting-edge technologies, such as AI, MR, cloud computing, and data analytics. By collaborating with industry partners, conducting extensive research and development, and providing a robust ecosystem of products and services, Microsoft empowers businesses and IT managers to stay ahead of the competition and adapt to rapidly evolving technological landscapes. Through this commitment, Microsoft enables organizations to transform their operations, enhance customer experiences, and drive growth by harnessing the full potential of digital innovation.

AI-powered tools

AI has emerged as a powerful tool for innovation across industries, revolutionizing how we approach problem-solving, decision-making, and strategic planning. Azure's robust suite of AI-powered tools is designed to help your organization use this transformative technology, ushering in new levels of efficiency, insight, and innovation.

Azure AI encompasses a variety of services and tools that cater to different AI needs, from Azure Machine Learning, which enables data scientists and developers to build, train, and deploy machine learning models, to Azure Cognitive Services, a collection of pre-trained AI services for vision, speech, language understanding, decision-making, and more. These tools democratize access to AI, enabling businesses of all sizes and sectors to adopt AI without requiring in-depth expertise.

AI-powered Azure tools can automate routine tasks, freeing your workforce to focus on more strategic and innovative projects. They can also deliver powerful predictive analytics, helping you anticipate market trends, customer needs, and business challenges. Furthermore, Azure's AI tools can enhance customer experiences, making interactions with your business more intuitive and personalized.

We've merely skimmed the surface of Microsoft's AI capabilities in this introductory section. To read more about the latest AI and machine learning updates in Azure, check out this link:

```
https://azure.microsoft.com/updates/?category=ai-machine-learning
```

Mixed reality

One of the cutting-edge trends in technology today that's gaining substantial traction in various industries is **Mixed Reality** (**MR**). This blend of the real and virtual worlds opens up new opportunities for business interaction, communication, and operational efficiency.

Microsoft Azure, always at the forefront of innovation, is leading the charge in exploring and applying MR. Through Azure, you can access Azure MR services, designed to help businesses create immersive and interactive experiences that transcend the barriers of time and location.

Consider, for instance, the possibility of creating a digital twin of a physical product or an environment. Engineers could interact with this virtual model in real time, enabling them to detect issues, make modifications, or predict failures before they occur in the physical world. Likewise, imagine the value of providing remote assistance through HoloLens 2, where an expert could guide a field technician through a complex process, step by step, without needing to be physically present.

In education and training, MR offers opportunities for experiential learning, where students can immerse themselves in the subject matter, resulting in a more engaging and effective learning experience. The possibilities for MR are indeed extensive and exciting.

To **learn more about MR, check out these URLs:**

- Azure Digital Twins: `https://azure.microsoft.com/products/digital-twins/`
- Spatial Anchors: `https://azure.microsoft.com/products/spatial-anchors/`
- Microsoft HoloLens 2: `https://www.microsoft.com/hololens`
- Azure Kinect DK: `https://azure.microsoft.com/products/kinect-dk/`
- Mixed Reality Toolkit 3: `https://learn.microsoft.com/windows/mixed-reality/mrtk-unity/mrtk3-overview/`

Quantum computing

Quantum computing holds a place of distinction in the realm of innovative technologies poised to revolutionize businesses. This exciting new field has the potential to solve complex problems that are currently beyond the capabilities of classical computers. Azure Quantum is Microsoft's full stack, open cloud ecosystem dedicated to quantum computing, and it presents unparalleled opportunities for business decision-makers.

Azure Quantum gives you access to diverse quantum resources, including pre-built solutions, quantum development tools, and quantum hardware from leading providers. This open approach empowers your business to experiment, learn, and build with the technology of the quantum era. As a result, Azure Quantum's potential for innovation spans many industries, from optimizing logistics and solving complex mathematical problems to creating new materials and drugs.

Consider, for example, the field of financial services. Here, quantum computing could enhance portfolio optimization, risk analysis, and fraud detection. In healthcare, Azure Quantum can pave the way for faster discovery of new drugs and better modeling of biological systems.

Integrating Azure Quantum into your business strategy could place you at the forefront of the quantum revolution. You can learn more about Azure Quantum here: `https://learn.microsoft.com/azure/quantum/`.

Thinking about cloud management, migration, security, and governance

As a business decision-maker or technical professional, it is essential to understand the importance of cloud management, migration, security, and governance when developing, evaluating, or adopting a cloud strategy. These aspects are critical in ensuring an organization's cloud environment is efficient, secure, and compliant with relevant regulations and policies. Let's briefly look at these areas.

Cost management

Effective cost management is a cornerstone of any successful cloud strategy. As a business decision-maker, understanding and controlling your cloud expenses is a crucial challenge. Microsoft Azure provides robust solutions for this very purpose. With its extensive suite of cost management tools, Azure can help your organization to better comprehend, optimize, and manage its cloud spending.

Azure's cost management tools allow increased visibility and control over your cloud spending, enabling you to make informed decisions about resource allocation and investment. This allows your organization to use the cloud more effectively, maximizing the benefits of your investment.

Azure also provides tools for setting budgets and monitoring spending. For example, you can create custom budgets for your cloud projects and receive alerts when spending approaches your predetermined thresholds.

Moreover, Azure's suite includes features to optimize resource utilization and take advantage of Reserved Instances and Savings Plans. These elements of Azure can help identify underutilized resources and lock in lower prices for services, respectively.

Ultimately, Azure's comprehensive cost management tools and resources help your organization optimize expenses, maintain control over costs, and reap the most value from your cloud investment.

In subsequent chapters of this book, we will expand upon each aspect of Azure's cost management capabilities, offering more profound insights into how these tools can be used to maximize your organization's operational efficiency and financial health in the cloud. By understanding these elements, you can implement an Azure strategy that aligns with your business needs and drives sustainable growth.

Migration and deployment

As more organizations transition toward cloud-based solutions, understanding the process of cloud migration and deployment becomes increasingly critical. With its robust and user-friendly features, Microsoft Azure provides an ideal platform for such a transition.

In the journey toward the cloud, Azure helps businesses effectively assess their readiness for migration. It offers tools to analyze your organization's infrastructure and systems, determining the most efficient and seamless path to the cloud.

Choosing the right cloud platform is another crucial decision in your cloud journey. Azure's flexible and scalable solutions cater to a wide variety of business needs, whether you require IaaS, PaaS, or SaaS solutions.

Executing a seamless deployment is another aspect where Azure shines. It provides an intuitive and robust set of tools for deploying and managing applications, databases, and services in the cloud, reducing time, cost, and complexity.

Successful migration to Azure can have significant benefits for your organization. It can boost operational efficiency, lay the groundwork for future growth, and enable your business to make use of new technologies and innovations. Furthermore, Azure's ongoing management and monitoring tools ensure that your cloud environment remains optimal and evolves with your business needs.

This introduction only scratches the surface of what Azure migration and deployment entail. In the following chapters of this book, we'll delve deeper into each stage of the migration and deployment process, providing comprehensive strategies and detailed guidance to ensure your transition to Azure is as smooth and beneficial as possible. Understanding these processes will be essential to implementing an effective Azure strategy and achieving your organization's objectives in the cloud.

Configuration management

Configuration management is an essential part of any cloud strategy, and Azure offers a host of tools to streamline this crucial process. It ensures the consistency of your cloud resources, maintains the system performance, and upholds the security of your cloud environment.

Azure's configuration management tools help monitor and automate your Azure resources' setup, configuration, and management. They enable your business to ensure consistency and compliance across your entire Azure environment, reducing the risk of errors and system outages due to misconfiguration.

Azure Automation State Configuration, for example, allows you to manage your Azure and non-Azure environments from a central location, defining and enforcing configurations across your cloud and on-premises systems.

The Azure Policy service, on the other hand, helps you create, assign, and manage policies to enforce rules and effects over your resources, ensuring compliance with corporate standards and SLAs.

Proper configuration management can improve system reliability, accelerate deployment processes, reduce downtime, and improve security, hence leading to considerable savings in time, costs, and resources.

The key to effective configuration management lies in understanding your organization's specific needs and aligning Azure's capabilities to those needs. However, the details and intricacies of configuration management in Azure are vast, which we will explore more thoroughly in subsequent chapters of this book. By comprehending these processes, you, as a business decision-maker, will be better equipped to use Azure's configuration management capabilities to maintain an efficient, reliable, and secure cloud environment.

Unified governance, risk management, and compliance

Unified governance, risk management, and compliance are indispensable aspects of Azure's strategy and implementation. Unified governance, risk management, and compliance in Azure provide a framework for aligning IT operations with business objectives, managing risk effectively, and meeting compliance requirements.

Azure offers robust tools and services that support unified governance, risk management, and compliance, aiding organizations in maintaining a secure and compliant state while managing risks efficiently. For example, Azure Policy helps enforce organizational standards and assess compliance at scale. Similarly, Azure Blueprints allows the quick creation of governed subscriptions to balance agility and control.

On the other hand, Microsoft Defender for Cloud and Azure Advisor provide proactive insights to manage risks effectively. They help protect your Azure resources, offer threat protection, and provide clear, actionable recommendations to optimize your Azure deployments.

For managing compliance, **Update management center** provides access to a portfolio of compliance offerings, making it easier for businesses to meet the complex regulatory requirements of their industry. In addition, it keeps you informed about how Microsoft protects your data and maintains compliance with global standards.

Unified governance, risk management, and compliance are paramount for any organization to establish effective controls, avoid fines for non-compliance, protect the organization from risk, and keep the business operations running smoothly. A comprehensive understanding of these components provides a strong foundation for successful Azure strategy and implementation.

However, the scope and intricacies of unified governance, risk management, and compliance in Azure are vast, which we will explore in the upcoming chapters. By comprehending these, you, as a business decision-maker, can confidently harness Azure's capabilities to ensure your cloud environment's security, compliance, and efficient risk management.

Observability and resiliency

In an increasingly complex and interconnected digital landscape, the concepts of observability and resiliency have become cornerstones of a successful Azure strategy and implementation.

Observability, in the context of Azure, encompasses the practices and tools that provide insight into your applications, infrastructure, and network, allowing you to understand the state of your systems, diagnose problems, and optimize performance. In addition, Azure provides a suite of services such as Azure Monitor, Azure Log Analytics, and Azure Application Insights that can gather, analyze, and visualize telemetry data from various sources, providing actionable insights about your application and infrastructure.

On the other hand, resiliency is about designing and operating your systems to withstand disruptions and recover quickly from any issues. Azure Site Recovery and Azure Backup provide vital capabilities to ensure business continuity and disaster recovery. Furthermore, Azure's globally distributed datacenters and services, such as Azure Traffic Manager, facilitate high availability and load balancing across regions.

Maintaining a balance between observability and resiliency is critical to managing complex cloud environments. These aspects enable you to maintain high performance and uptime, mitigate risks, and quickly respond to changes or disruptions.

However, it is essential to acknowledge the breadth and depth of these concepts. Hence, we will delve into these topics more deeply in subsequent chapters, equipping you as a business decision-maker with a thorough understanding of Azure's observability and resiliency capabilities and enabling you to design and implement robust, resilient, and observable solutions in Azure.

Security and control

Security and control remain paramount as business decision-makers strategize and implement Azure-based solutions. As a result, Azure, Microsoft's flagship cloud offering, is built with a robust security model to ensure data protection, privacy, and compliance.

Azure offers a multitude of features and services that form a multi-layered security architecture. Azure Active Directory for identity and access management, Microsoft Defender for Cloud for unified security management, and Azure Key Vault for securely storing application secrets are just a few examples of the security services available. These capabilities help safeguard your organization's assets, manage identities, detect threats, and respond effectively to incidents.

However, security is not just about protection but also about control. Azure provides granular control over your resources with features such as **role-based access control** (**RBAC**), policy enforcement, and resource locks. These mechanisms allow you to decide who has access to your resources, what actions they can perform, and under what conditions.

A firm grip on security and control is a prerequisite for achieving an effective Azure strategy and implementation. However, comprehending the breadth and depth of these domains in Azure requires a deeper dive. Subsequent chapters in this book will delve further into these topics, providing a comprehensive understanding of Azure's security and control features and enabling you to build, deploy, and manage secure and well-governed applications and infrastructures on Azure.

Bringing it all together

All the concepts covered in this section, such as cost management, migration, deployment, configuration management, governance, risk management, compliance, observability, resiliency, and security, often overlap because they all contribute to the successful operation, management, and maintenance of cloud resources and applications. Ensuring that these concepts work cohesively to provide a seamless experience for the user, regardless of the deployment model from cloud to edge, is referred to as unified operations. We will be discussing unified operations in more detail in the next chapter.

Start building with Azure

Embarking on your journey with Azure opens up a world of possibilities for your organization. By making use of the power of Azure's cutting-edge cloud technology, you can drive innovation, increase efficiency, and improve scalability. Azure offers a comprehensive suite of services tailored to address various business requirements, from data storage and analytics to application development and deployment. With robust security, compliance, and governance tools built in, you can confidently trust Azure to protect your valuable assets. Whether you're a small start-up or a large enterprise, Azure's flexible and cost-effective solutions can help you stay ahead of the competition. Don't miss out on this opportunity to transform your organization's IT infrastructure; start exploring Azure today and unlock your business's full potential.

Here are eight steps you should consider for embarking on your Azure journey:

1. **Learn about Azure**: Read this book, then research Azure services and offerings to understand how they align with your organization's needs. Visit the Azure website, read documentation, and explore use cases to gain insights into how Azure can benefit your business.

2. **Sign up for a free trial**: Azure offers a 12-month free trial with $200 credit to explore and test Azure services. Sign up at the Azure portal (`https://portal.azure.com`) using your business email address to create an account and take advantage of the free trial.

3. **Evaluate your current infrastructure**: Assess your existing IT environment, including applications, workloads, and data storage requirements. This will help you identify which Azure services are most relevant to your organization's needs and set priorities for migration.

4. **Plan your migration**: Develop a migration plan that outlines the steps for moving your applications, workloads, and data to Azure. Consider factors such as security, compliance, and cost optimization. In addition, you may want to use Azure Migrate, a service that helps assess and migrate on-premises workloads to Azure.

5. **Engage with a partner or Microsoft representative**: Consult with Microsoft representatives or Azure partners for expert advice on best practices and strategies for a successful migration. They can help you with architecture, planning, and implementation.

6. **Train your team**: Ensure your IT staff and other relevant personnel are well trained in Azure technologies. Microsoft Learn provides no-cost, self-paced learning paths for various Azure services and roles, while Microsoft certifications offer comprehensive skill validation.

7. **Implement governance and security**: Establish and enforce security, compliance, and governance policies using Azure services such as Azure Policy, Azure Blueprints, and Azure Security Center.

8. **Monitor and optimize**: Once your resources are deployed in Azure, continuously monitor performance, security, and cost. Use Azure Monitor, Azure Cost Management, and Azure Advisor to gain insights and optimize your cloud environment.

By following these steps, your organization can smoothly transition to Azure and unlock the potential of cloud computing for improved efficiency, scalability, and innovation.

Summary

We've concluded our introductory chapter, but this is just the beginning of our journey. In this chapter, we scratched the surface of the vast and dynamic landscape of cloud computing, and its continually evolving models. After that, we outlined the compelling reasons for adopting Microsoft Azure, driven by its powerful features and capabilities.

We also touched upon the various types of cloud environments—public and private clouds, hybrid cloud, multicloud, and even the emerging field of edge computing. Each of these comes with its own unique set of benefits and considerations, providing diverse solutions tailored to an organization's specific needs.

A pivotal aspect of our discussion involved delving into some crucial considerations for businesses transitioning to Azure—cloud management, migration, security, and governance. These complex aspects are the bedrock of any successful Azure strategy and require careful planning and execution.

As we progress through the rest of the book, we'll dive deeper into these critical areas. We'll expand on the broad topics here, providing a more detailed understanding to empower you to make informed, strategic decisions for your organization's Azure journey.

The journey ahead will require strategic thinking, sound decision-making, and a keen understanding of your organization's needs. With this knowledge, you'll be well equipped to use Azure's robust capabilities to your advantage, driving your organization's innovation, efficiency, and growth.

So, buckle up and get ready to dive deeper. The world of Azure awaits, promising exciting insights, powerful tools, and transformative opportunities. Here's to a fruitful journey toward cloud mastery with Azure!

2
Modernizing with Hybrid, Multicloud, and Edge Computing

As a business decision-maker in IT, you might question the need for various cloud computing models, such as hybrid cloud, multicloud, and edge computing. The key lies in understanding that these diverse models serve unique purposes, catering to different business objectives and technical requirements.

The hybrid cloud model blends private and public cloud infrastructures. By utilizing public cloud services, organizations can scale cost effectively. On the other hand, sensitive data and applications can remain on the private cloud infrastructure, preserving control where needed. This balanced approach allows organizations to integrate seamlessly and encourages cooperation across the organization.

The multicloud strategy enables organizations to utilize multiple cloud service providers to meet diverse business objectives. This approach frees businesses from the constraints of a single vendor, enabling them to avail themselves of each provider's unique strengths. Distributing workloads across different cloud environments enables an organization to balance performance, security and regulatory requirements, and maintain flexibility.

Edge computing, on the other hand, addresses the need for speed and efficiency in data processing. Organizations can reduce latency, improve response times, and optimize bandwidth usage by bringing computation and data storage closer to the data generation source. This is particularly beneficial for applications requiring real-time processing or operating in remote locations with limited connectivity.

Having different cloud computing models is not a case of redundancy but a strategic response to an organization's wide range of needs. Whether it's the need for control and security, flexibility and cost optimization, or speed and efficiency, a cloud model is designed to address it. Understanding the strengths and benefits of hybrid cloud, multicloud, and edge computing allows your organization to build an optimized cloud strategy to encourage growth, drive innovation, and maintain a competitive edge.

In this chapter, we will cover the following topics:

- Comparison between hybrid, multicloud and edge computing
- Use cases and considerations for various cloud models
- Reference architecture for Microsoft Azure
- Operational and technical considerations when adopting Azure

Reasons for embracing hybrid, multicloud, and edge computing

Embracing hybrid cloud, multicloud, and edge computing strategies allows businesses to optimize IT resources, drive innovation, and maintain a competitive edge in an increasingly digital landscape. A thoughtfully designed hybrid cloud environment offers an adaptable, secure, and cost-effective infrastructure that aligns with your strategic objectives and operational requirements while considering your organization's unique demands in control, security, scalability, cost efficiency, and compliance. Multicloud strategies enable businesses to avoid vendor lock-in, improve reliability, and capitalize on the unique offerings of each provider. At the same time, edge computing enhances user experiences and operational efficiency by enabling real-time processing, low latency, and optimized bandwidth usage. Together, these approaches empower organizations to achieve the desired business outcomes, such as increased agility, enhanced customer satisfaction, and streamlined operations, all while effectively managing and mitigating risks associated with data management, regulatory compliance, and technological advancements.

Motivations and business outcomes

Embracing hybrid cloud, multicloud, and edge computing strategies can improve various areas of a business, addressing specific motivations and aligning with organizational goals:

- The hybrid cloud model offers a balanced approach by combining a private cloud's robust security, control, and compliance with the cost efficiency and scalability offered by public cloud services. By creating an integrated environment, businesses can optimize IT resources based on specific workload requirements, ensure seamless collaboration, and maintain high-level data security. This strategy safeguards sensitive data and complies with regulatory requirements to achieve cost efficiencies and enhance operational agility.

- Multicloud allows businesses to diversify risk and embrace the strengths of various cloud providers. Businesses adopt multicloud strategies with the motivation to balance performance, security, and regulatory requirements. A multicloud strategy helps organizations avoid vendor lock-in, enhances reliability, and capitalizes on unique offerings from multiple cloud service providers.

- Edge computing enables the **Internet of Things** (**IoT**) and high-demand, real-time applications for organizations that require faster response times, lower latency, and more efficient operations. Edge computing allows data processing and storage to occur closer to the source of data generation, such as IoT devices or end users. This results in real-time or near real-time insights, enhanced user experiences, and less strain on central and cloud-based systems. Edge computing also facilitates operation in remote locations with limited connectivity, supporting the scalability and reach of your organization.

The flexibility and scalability offered by hybrid, multicloud, and edge computing solutions enable organizations to rapidly develop, test, and deploy new products and services, fostering innovation and driving growth. By recognizing and addressing the specific motivations of these different areas, you can strategically embrace hybrid, multicloud, and edge computing solutions to enhance overall organizational performance and achieve the desired business outcomes.

Additional considerations

In today's rapidly evolving digital landscape, hybrid cloud, multicloud, and edge computing are at the forefront of strategic discussions among business decision-makers. These powerful paradigms shape how organizations drive efficiency, foster innovation, and maintain a competitive edge. Here are some key considerations to consider when evaluating a cloud strategy. These considerations span various dimensions—from cost optimization and business agility to data management, customer experience, and environmental responsibility. Understanding these factors will provide a comprehensive insight into the motivations and desired business outcomes of adopting hybrid, multicloud, and edge computing strategies, enabling decision-makers to make more informed choices that align with their organizational objectives and vision:

- **Cost optimization**: Ensuring the cost-effectiveness of the chosen cloud services to support the organization's financial health.

- **Agility**: Maintaining an agile infrastructure that can adapt rapidly to changing business needs across various departments.

- **Risk management**: Mitigating potential risks from outages, failures, or data breaches to protect the business and its operations.

- **Innovation**: Empowering the faster deployment of new applications and services to drive organizational innovation.

- **Compliance**: Achieving regulatory and compliance requirements by hosting sensitive data on private clouds and non-sensitive data on public clouds.

- **Scalability**: The capability to handle growth and peak workloads is critical for driving business expansion.

- **Data management**: Ensuring the ability to manage and analyze large volumes of data from multiple sources is critical in informed decision-making.

- **Collaboration:** Facilitating efficient collaboration across teams in different regions with a unified platform for sharing data and resources.

- **Customer experience**: Improving customer interactions through data analysis and targeted marketing campaigns, enhancing customer satisfaction and loyalty.

- **Environmental responsibility**: Balancing business needs with environmental consciousness by reducing energy consumption and carbon footprint, minimizing waste, and maximizing renewable energy sources through your choice of cloud providers.

As businesses recognize the benefits of embracing hybrid, multicloud, and edge computing strategies, it becomes imperative to establish a cohesive approach to managing these diverse and interconnected environments. Enter unified operations, which bridges the gap between these technologies, enabling organizations to optimize resource allocation, improve operational efficiency, and drive innovation. By seamlessly integrating hybrid, multicloud, and edge environments, unified operations empower organizations to capitalize on each computing approach's unique strengths and capabilities while maintaining data security and compliance. This transition to unified operations ensures that businesses can effectively engage with modern cloud computing models and edge technologies, positioning themselves for success in an ever-evolving digital landscape.

What makes a hybrid, multicloud, and edge strategy successful?

As the digital landscape evolves, adopting hybrid, multicloud, and edge computing strategies has become crucial for businesses seeking to maintain a competitive edge and drive innovation. However, to fully explore the potential of these technologies, it is essential to understand the factors that contribute to their successful implementation. Here, we will outline the key elements that make a hybrid, multicloud, and edge strategy successful, enabling you to make informed decisions and effectively position your organization for growth in today's dynamic business environment.

Identifying and addressing concerns

Each model has specific concerns that should be addressed when evaluating its suitability for a business. Here are some of the concerns to consider.

Hybrid cloud

- **Integration**: Ensuring seamless integration between on-premises and cloud resources can be challenging. Focus on interoperability, unified management, and consistent APIs.

- **Data security**: Safeguarding sensitive data between private and public clouds is essential. Implement strong encryption and access control measures.

- **Vendor lock-in**: Avoid becoming overly reliant on a single cloud provider, which can limit flexibility and control over the infrastructure.

Multicloud

- **Complexity**: Managing multiple cloud providers and platforms increases complexity. Consider using a centralized management solution to streamline operations.

- **Data transfer costs**: Transferring data between cloud providers can incur additional costs. Optimize data flow to minimize expenses.

- **Consistency**: Maintaining consistent security, governance, and operational policies across multiple clouds is crucial. Develop a unified strategy that aligns with business objectives.

Edge computing

- **Device security**: Protecting edge devices and IoT systems from potential breaches is vital. Regularly update and patch devices to address vulnerabilities.

- **Network latency**: Ensuring low latency for real-time data processing requires efficient data management and optimized network architecture.

- **Distributed management**: Managing distributed edge nodes can be challenging. Implement automated orchestration and monitoring tools to maintain system performance and resilience.

Addressing these concerns for hybrid, multicloud, and edge computing models can help businesses optimize their infrastructure while mitigating potential risks and challenges. When evaluating these three options, the following steps can help guide you in this process:

1. **Assess your organization's needs**: Begin by evaluating your organization's specific needs, requirements, and objectives. Next, understand the nature of your workloads, data sensitivity, and regulatory compliance requirements to determine the most appropriate mix of hybrid, multicloud, and edge computing solutions.

2. **Develop a comprehensive strategy**: Create a well-defined plan that outlines your organization's approach to adopting and integrating these technologies. Consider data management, security, connectivity, and cost compatibility to ensure seamless and efficient operations.

3. **Establish clear governance and policies**: Develop robust governance structures and policies to manage data, applications, and infrastructure across multiple environments. This includes data privacy, access controls, and compliance with industry standards and regulations.

4. **Invest in the right skill set**: As you adopt these new technologies, ensure your IT staff has the necessary skills and expertise. Provide training, hire new talent, or partner with external experts to fill any knowledge gaps and facilitate a successful implementation.

5. **Choose reliable partners**: Select cloud service providers and technology partners with a proven track record of delivering reliable, secure, and compliant solutions. Evaluate their offerings, performance, and support capabilities to ensure they align with your organization's needs and objectives.

6. **Monitor and optimize**: Continuously monitor the performance, security, and cost-efficiency of your hybrid, multicloud, and edge computing environments. Use analytics and automation tools to identify areas for improvement and optimize resources based on changing business needs.

Communicating with and engaging stakeholders

Keep all relevant stakeholders informed about the benefits, risks, and progress of your hybrid, multicloud, and edge computing initiatives. Address concerns and ensure employees understand their roles and responsibilities in this new environment.

By taking these steps, you can proactively address potential concerns and ensure your organization successfully adopts hybrid cloud, multicloud, and edge computing strategies. This, in turn, will enable you to achieve your desired business outcomes, drive innovation, and maintain a competitive advantage in the digital landscape.

How Microsoft Azure helps?

As you explore the process of identifying and addressing concerns related to adopting hybrid cloud, multicloud, and edge computing strategies, selecting a technology platform partner that can help you navigate the complexities of these environments while providing the necessary tools and support is crucial. Microsoft Azure, a leading cloud services platform, offers a wide range of solutions designed to alleviate concerns associated with these strategies, providing your organization with a secure, reliable, and flexible foundation for digital transformation.

Adopting a hybrid cloud strategy with Azure can alleviate concerns by providing seamless and secure integration between your on-premises infrastructure and the Azure public cloud. In addition, Azure offers a comprehensive suite of services and tools, such as Azure Arc and Azure Stack, enabling organizations to extend Azure capabilities to their on-premises data centers. This ensures a consistent management experience, streamlined governance, and compliance across both environments, allowing you to maintain control over sensitive data while benefiting from the scalability and cost efficiency of the public cloud.

Vendor lock-in and concerns

Vendor lock-in occurs when an organization becomes overly reliant on a single cloud service provider to the extent that switching to a different provider becomes costly, complex, and time-consuming. The risks associated with vendor lock-in include limited flexibility, dependence on a vendor's pricing changes, lack of innovation due to reduced competition, and potential disruption in services if the vendor encounters issues.

Azure has multicloud capabilities that can play a pivotal role in mitigating these concerns. Embracing a multicloud strategy facilitated by Azure enables an organization to use multiple cloud providers' unique strengths and offerings. Azure supports interoperability and integration with other leading cloud platforms. This allows your organization to build and deploy applications using the best features from each provider, further reducing the risk associated with vendor lock-in.

Importantly, the robust security and compliance features of Azure maintain high data protection and regulatory compliance levels, regardless of the cloud providers you partner with. This means that even while diversifying your cloud portfolio, you can remain confident that your data's security and regulatory obligations are being effectively managed.

Overcome latency, bandwidth, and data processing concerns in remote locations

Businesses often find it difficult to manage data and application performance in remote locations. A key part of this is latency (the delay between sending and receiving data), bandwidth (the volume of data that can be transmitted over a network), and the processing of large volumes of data generated at these locations. These factors can impact the performance of applications, the quality of user experiences, and the efficiency of business operations.

Azure includes edge computing solutions, such as Azure IoT Edge and Azure Stack Edge, that are designed to address these challenges head-on. By processing data at the edge of the network – that is, closer to where it is generated – organizations can significantly reduce latency, improve response times, and optimize bandwidth usage. For example, a business with operations spread across multiple locations might need to process vast amounts of data in real time for decision-making or operational efficiency. Azure edge computing solutions enable real-time data processing at the source, vastly reducing latency, and ensuring quick and accurate business decisions.

Edge computing can help manage bandwidth constraints. As a result, businesses can efficiently use their network bandwidth by processing data locally and only transmitting necessary information to the cloud, reducing costs and avoiding network congestion. In addition, Azure offers comprehensive security features and centralized management tools that provide data protection and regulatory compliance at the edge, enabling your organization to get the benefits of edge computing without compromising on security or control.

Mapping strategic intentions

As an IT business decision-maker, strategic planning is critical when considering hybrid cloud, multicloud, and edge computing projects. Having a clear vision of what you want to achieve will guide your decisions and allow you to measure success effectively. Here are some considerations to guide your strategic intentions:

1. Firstly, understand your organization's needs and goals. For example, do you need to improve flexibility and scalability to handle varying workloads? Are you looking to optimize costs or enhance data security and compliance? Understanding your primary objectives will help you decide whether a hybrid cloud, multicloud, or edge computing strategy, or a combination, is right for your organization.

2. When mapping your strategic intentions, it's crucial to consider your current IT infrastructure, the skills and expertise within your organization, and the potential financial implications. Remember that a clear roadmap, a robust governance model, and an emphasis on security are all critical success factors in hybrid cloud, multicloud, and edge computing initiatives. Take the time to understand your needs, evaluate your options, and craft a strategy that aligns with your business goals, and you'll be well on your way to a successful transformation.

3. Establishing a successful hybrid cloud, multicloud, and edge computing strategy requires a holistic approach. Identify and address specific concerns associated with each approach.

4. Open communication and engagement with all relevant stakeholders are crucial. As we've seen, this includes the IT team, business leaders, and other key decision-makers within the organization. This ensures that the implemented solutions align with the overall business goals and helps foster a culture of buy-in and shared responsibility.

5. Microsoft Azure emerges as a strong ally in these strategic efforts. Its robust features and capabilities, including interoperability with other cloud platforms and edge computing solutions, are designed to address the common challenges organizations face in these areas.

6. With a multicloud strategy, organizations can avoid vendor lock-in constraints, promoting resilience, flexibility, and cost optimization. Similarly, edge computing addresses the challenges of latency, bandwidth, and data processing in remote locations. By shifting computation closer to the source of data generation, edge computing offers tangible benefits regarding response times, operational efficiency, and user experiences.

7. Lastly, mapping strategic intentions for your hybrid cloud, multicloud, and edge computing projects is pivotal. This exercise ensures that your technology strategies align with your business objectives, providing a clear roadmap toward successful implementation.

A successful hybrid, multicloud, and edge strategy is multifaceted. It encompasses careful consideration, strategic planning, and effective execution. By keeping these factors in mind, your organization will be well positioned to seize the opportunities these technologies offer, all while managing risk and fostering innovation in an increasingly digital business landscape.

Unified operations – one set of tools and processes

In an increasingly digitized and distributed IT landscape, unified operations form the cornerstone of efficient and effective IT management. Microsoft Azure equips business decision-makers with comprehensive tools and capabilities to streamline and centralize operations across diverse environments.

Implementing unified operations in hybrid, multicloud, and edge computing environments is fundamental to maintaining control, simplifying management, and optimizing efficiency. Using the extensive suite of tools and services in Azure, businesses can integrate and manage their diverse IT resources from a single pane, fostering a seamless operational experience across the entire infrastructure:

- In a hybrid cloud setup, Azure offers services such as Azure Arc, which allows businesses to manage their on-premises and multicloud resources seamlessly from a single control plane. This ensures consistency in management and governance across your entire IT infrastructure. Azure Stack also brings Azure services into your on-premises data center, allowing for integrated and streamlined operations between your on-site and cloud resources.

- For multicloud environments, the interoperability Azure offers is vital. With its broad set of connectors, APIs, and SDKs, Azure can interact effectively with other major cloud service providers, enabling centralized management across different clouds. This simplifies operations, reduces administrative overhead, and fosters a vendor-agnostic IT landscape.

- Azure provides services such as Azure IoT Edge and Azure Stack Edge, which extend cloud management and analytics capabilities to edge devices. This allows for a uniform operational model across your central cloud and edge locations, simplifying management and improving efficiency.

Furthermore, the advanced AI and machine learning capabilities in Azure provide insightful analytics and automated remediation, enhancing operational efficiency. Tools such as Azure Monitor and Azure Advisor offer real-time insights into your infrastructure, identify issues, and suggest best practices to optimize resources and operations.

An organization must adopt a strategic approach to truly achieve unified operations. This includes ensuring your teams have the necessary skills and training, your processes are designed to support unified operations, and your business culture embraces change. Through a strategic approach and the advanced tooling Azure offers, unified operations can deliver significant benefits, including reduced costs, improved efficiency, and enhanced agility for your business.

Key impacts

The key impacts of unified operations are evident in the way organizations become more responsive, efficient, and competitive in today's digital landscape. By providing a single, cohesive platform for managing IT resources, businesses can eliminate silos, streamline operations, and enhance the overall effectiveness of their technology investments. Moreover, unified operations enable organizations to capitalize on the unique strengths and capabilities of hybrid, multicloud, and edge computing solutions, ensuring that they stay at the forefront of innovation and maintain a competitive advantage in an increasingly interconnected and dynamic world.

While the generalized key impacts of unified operations, such as improved operational efficiency, cost optimization, and increased agility, apply to a wide range of industries, it is essential to recognize how these impacts manifest uniquely within specific sectors. By examining the distinctive needs, challenges, and opportunities faced by key industries, such as healthcare, finance, manufacturing, retail, energy, telecommunications, and construction, we can better understand the tangible benefits and transformative potential that unified operations brings to each of these sectors. In doing so, business decision-makers can tailor their approach to implementing unified operations, ensuring they fully engage with this cohesive IT management strategy to drive industry-specific innovation and growth:

1. **Healthcare organizations**: Unified operations can help organizations manage patient data, medical records, and complex applications securely and efficiently across various computing environments. This enables better collaboration among healthcare providers, improved patient care, and compliance with stringent data protection regulations.

2. **Financial institutions**: Financial institutions can use unified operations to optimize IT infrastructure, maintain regulatory compliance, and manage sensitive data across hybrid, multicloud, and edge environments. This improves risk management, cost optimization, and enhanced customer experiences.

3. **Manufacturers**: Manufacturers can use unified operations to monitor and control production processes, manage supply chains, and optimize logistics in real time. The seamless integration of hybrid, multicloud, and edge computing solutions enables better decision-making, increased operational efficiency, and accelerated innovation.

4. **Retail businesses**: Unified operations can help retailers enhance customer experiences, optimize inventory management, and streamline supply chain processes by integrating data and applications across multiple environments. This allows retailers to deliver personalized shopping experiences, improve operational efficiency, and drive growth.

5. **Energy companies**: Energy companies can use unified operations to manage data, applications, and infrastructure across their diverse computing environments, enabling better monitoring and control of energy production, distribution, and consumption. This fosters efficient resource allocation, improved sustainability, and compliance with regulatory requirements.

6. **Telecommunication providers**: Telecommunication providers can use unified operations to efficiently manage network infrastructure, data, and applications across hybrid, multicloud, and edge environments. This ensures optimal network performance, enhanced customer experiences, and streamlined service delivery.

These are just a few examples of industries that can engage with unified operations to drive efficiency, innovation, and growth. Organizations across various sectors can achieve their strategic objectives and maintain a competitive advantage in an increasingly digital world by implementing a cohesive approach to managing IT resources across hybrid, multicloud, and edge computing environments.

Thinking about workloads and architecture

Understanding the factors contributing to a successful hybrid, multicloud, and edge strategy is the first step toward adopting these innovative technologies. However, it is also crucial to consider your organization's specific workloads and architecture to ensure a seamless transition and maximize the benefits of these computing environments. By shifting the focus from the general success factors to a more detailed examination of your organization's workloads and architecture, you can tailor your approach to implementing hybrid, multicloud, and edge computing. This enables you to create a more resilient, scalable, and efficient IT infrastructure that meets your unique business needs and drives innovation, agility, and growth in an increasingly digital landscape.

Use cases and technical considerations

After carefully assessing the workloads and architecture of your organization, it is essential to delve deeper into specific use cases and technical considerations that can guide the successful implementation of hybrid, multicloud, and edge computing strategies. By exploring practical applications of these technologies and understanding the key factors that influence their performance, security, and cost-effectiveness, you can make well-informed decisions about deploying and optimizing these innovative solutions within your organization.

Hybrid cloud

Data storage and backup

Hybrid cloud data storage and backup represent powerful tools for business decision-makers seeking to ensure data safety, continuity, and regulatory compliance while maintaining cost-effectiveness.

In a hybrid cloud model, you can store sensitive or mission-critical data on-premises within your private cloud, ensuring maximum control and enhanced security measures. This is especially beneficial in sectors with strict data regulations, such as healthcare or financial services.

Meanwhile, non-sensitive data or redundant backups can be stored on a public cloud, to make the most of the scalability and cost-effectiveness of the public cloud. This is particularly useful for managing large volumes of data or handling peak load periods. In addition, public cloud providers typically offer pay-as-you-go models, which means you only pay for the storage capacity you use.

Moreover, the hybrid cloud model supports effective disaster recovery strategies. By duplicating data and applications across private and public cloud environments, you can ensure business continuity even in an outage, hardware failure, or disaster scenario.

Thus, the flexibility, security, cost efficiency, and resilience offered by a hybrid cloud approach make it an ideal solution for data storage and backup, helping organizations balance their operational requirements, risk management concerns, and budget constraints.

Application development and testing

The hybrid cloud model presents significant application development and testing opportunities, offering a flexible and efficient environment that can drastically accelerate the development lifecycle and improve product quality for businesses.

In a hybrid cloud setting, developers can use public cloud platforms' vast resources and services for development and testing. This includes the rapid provisioning of development and testing environments, access to advanced development tools, and scaling resources up or down based on project requirements. This flexibility accelerates the development process, enhances team productivity, and reduces the need for significant up-front investments in infrastructure.

At the same time, sensitive elements, such as proprietary code, critical development data, or confidential customer information, can be securely managed in the private cloud, maintaining compliance with data security regulations and corporate policies.

Once the application is ready for deployment, it can be rolled out either on the private cloud for internal use or the public cloud for customer-facing scenarios, depending on the organization's needs.

Thus, using a hybrid cloud model for application development and testing offers businesses the best of both worlds, combining the agility and scalability of public cloud platforms with the security and control of private cloud infrastructure. This powerful combination can significantly enhance the efficiency and effectiveness of your organization's application development efforts.

High-performance computing

High-performance computing (HPC) in a hybrid cloud environment offers a powerful solution to meet the demands of compute-intensive tasks that businesses frequently encounter. Such tasks could range from complex simulations and data analytics to machine learning and AI workloads.

In a hybrid cloud setup, HPC workloads can be managed to balance cost-effectiveness, performance, and security. The public cloud component of a hybrid model offers vast resources and scalable computing power to handle peak loads or sporadic high-compute demands. This scalability is crucial for businesses that experience fluctuating needs, allowing them to avoid over-provisioning resources and thus saving on costs.

Simultaneously, sensitive datasets or proprietary algorithms that require stringent security controls can be kept on-premises or in the private cloud segment. This ensures the business maintains the necessary control and compliance over sensitive data and intellectual property.

Furthermore, a hybrid approach can provide enhanced resilience for HPC workloads. For example, if there are outages or disruptions in one part of the infrastructure, the workload can be shifted to other regions, thereby ensuring the continuity of operations.

By using hybrid cloud for HPC, businesses can take advantage of both on-demand scalability and enhanced security, leading to improved performance, increased flexibility, and potential cost savings.

Regulatory compliance

Regulatory compliance in a hybrid cloud environment provides an effective way for businesses to balance the need for innovation, efficiency, and adherence to relevant regulations. Various industries are bound by strict data handling, privacy, and security rules, such as the healthcare industry with HIPAA or financial services with GDPR, PCI-DSS, and other national regulations.

In a hybrid cloud setup, organizations can strategically allocate resources based on their sensitivity and compliance requirements. For example, **personally identifiable information (PII)** or other sensitive data can be stored and processed on private clouds or on-premise systems, allowing for tighter control, security, and compliance.

Conversely, non-sensitive workloads and data that do not require such stringent control can be deployed on public clouds, to take advantage of these services' scalability and cost-effectiveness. This dual approach ensures regulatory compliance and optimizes resource allocation based on the specific needs of each workload.

In addition, hybrid cloud providers such as Azure offer robust security and compliance features, including data encryption, identity and access management, and regular security audits. They also provide compliance certifications, validating their services' adherence to global and industry-specific compliance standards. As a result, businesses can effectively meet their obligations by using a hybrid cloud for regulatory compliance while driving innovation and growth.

Multicloud

Best-of-breed services

Organizations can take advantage of the best services and features from multiple cloud providers, selecting the most suitable solution for each workload and business requirement.

Selecting best-of-breed services in a multicloud environment involves identifying and incorporating specialized solutions from various cloud providers that best meet your organization's needs. First, evaluate each cloud platform's unique strengths and capabilities and choose services that align with your business objectives and requirements. Then, ensure seamless integration and compatibility across the platforms, using tools and services that facilitate management and governance across multiple cloud environments. By strategically selecting best-of-breed services, you can optimize performance, functionality, and innovation while maintaining flexibility in your multicloud architecture.

Azure empowers organizations to build a best-of-breed multicloud strategy by providing a wide range of advanced services, tools, and integrations that complement and enhance the capabilities of other cloud providers. For example, with Azure Arc, organizations can extend the management and governance capabilities of Azure to workloads running on other cloud platforms, such as AWS and Google Cloud, enabling a consistent and unified approach across multiple environments. Azure also offers seamless integration with popular third-party services and tools through its extensive marketplace, allowing organizations to incorporate specialized solutions from various vendors into their multicloud architecture. By combining the interoperability, hybrid capabilities, and strong partnerships that Azure offers with other technology leaders, businesses can create a tailored multicloud environment that aligns with their unique requirements, drives innovation, and optimizes performance, cost, and flexibility.

Optimizing costs

By using different cloud providers' unique pricing models and services in the right situations, organizations can optimize costs by selecting the most cost-effective solution for each workload.

Optimizing costs in a multicloud environment involves evaluating and managing expenses across different cloud platforms. Consider using cost management tools that provide visibility of your organization's cloud spending and usage patterns, helping identify areas for cost reduction and resource optimization. Also, assess the various pricing options available, such as pay-as-you-go, reserved instances, and spot instances, to choose the most cost-effective solutions for your workloads. By actively monitoring and managing your multicloud expenses, you can ensure efficient resource allocation, control costs, and maximize your return on investment.

Azure addresses cost optimization in multicloud environments by offering a comprehensive suite of tools and services that help organizations monitor, analyze, and manage their cloud expenses across different platforms. With Azure Cost Management, businesses can gain insights into their spending patterns, identify inefficiencies, and implement cost-saving measures across Azure, AWS, and Google Cloud. Azure Advisor also provides personalized recommendations to optimize resource usage, reduce costs, and improve performance across multiple cloud environments. Additionally, Azure offers flexible pricing options, such as pay-as-you-go, reserved instances, and spot instances, allowing organizations to choose the most cost-effective solutions for their workloads. By utilizing the robust cost management capabilities Azure offers, businesses can effectively navigate the complexities of multicloud cost optimization, ensuring they maximize the value of their cloud investments.

Geographic reach

Multicloud allows organizations to choose cloud providers with data centers in specific regions, ensuring low latency and compliance with local data residency regulations.

It's essential to consider the geographic reach of cloud providers in a multicloud environment. Evaluate each provider's data center locations, availability zones, and network performance to ensure low-latency access and improved user experience for your customers worldwide. Also, assess the provider's compliance with data residency and sovereignty requirements, ensuring sensitive data remains within desired geographic boundaries. By strategically selecting cloud providers with an extensive global presence, your organization can expand its reach, enhance performance, and meet the diverse needs of customers and stakeholders across the globe.

Azure enhances geographic reach in multicloud environments by offering a global network of data centers and an expansive range of connectivity options. With more than 60 regions worldwide, Azure enables organizations to deploy workloads and store data in locations that meet their specific latency, data residency, and compliance requirements. Businesses can use Azure ExpressRoute or VPN Gateway to establish private, high-speed connections between their on-premises infrastructure, Azure, and other cloud providers, ensuring optimal network performance across multiple environments. Furthermore, Azure Front Door and Azure **Content Delivery Network** (**CDN**) enhance global application delivery, providing faster response times and improved reliability for users worldwide. With the vast geographic reach and advanced networking capabilities of Azure, organizations can create a multicloud strategy that supports their global presence while meeting the diverse needs of their customers and stakeholders.

Avoiding vendor lock-in

Multicloud enables organizations to distribute workloads and data across multiple cloud providers, reducing reliance on a single vendor and fostering a flexible and agile IT environment.

Avoiding vendor lock-in in a multicloud environment involves selecting solutions that ensure flexibility and seamless integration across different cloud platforms. Prioritize support for open standards, interoperability, and widely used programming languages, frameworks, and tools to facilitate workload migration and compatibility. Consider management and governance services that extend across multiple cloud environments, allowing you to maintain consistent policies and controls. By focusing on these technical considerations, you can maximize your organization's freedom to adapt and evolve, making the most of your investments in the rapidly changing cloud landscape.

Azure supports avoiding vendor lock-in for multicloud environments by providing a flexible and open platform that allows organizations to distribute workloads and data across multiple cloud providers seamlessly. With Azure Arc, businesses can manage and govern resources on Azure and other cloud platforms, such as AWS and Google Cloud, enabling a consistent and unified management approach across diverse environments. In addition, Azure is commited to open standards, interoperability, and support for popular programming languages, frameworks, and tools, which ensures that organizations can easily integrate and migrate workloads between various cloud providers. By offering a comprehensive set of services, tools, and integrations that facilitate multicloud adoption, Azure empowers businesses to create a flexible and agile IT infrastructure that reduces reliance on a single vendor and allows them to use the best services and features from different cloud providers to meet their unique requirements.

Edge computing

Real-time data processing

In an era where immediacy is increasingly the norm, the ability to process data in real time has become a critical asset for many businesses. Edge computing is uniquely suited to meet this demand. By moving the data processing capabilities closer to the source of data generation—be it IoT devices, sensors, or end users—edge computing dramatically reduces the time it takes to analyze and act upon data. For instance, in industries such as manufacturing or healthcare, real-time data processing can mean the difference between catching a malfunctioning machine part before it causes downtime or detecting a patient's deteriorating condition before it becomes critical. In retail, it can enable personalized customer experiences through real-time targeted offers. By embracing edge computing, businesses can make decisions faster, mitigate risks more effectively, and provide responsive, personalized customer experiences, improving operational efficiency and customer satisfaction. Furthermore, real-time data processing at the edge also reduces the bandwidth requirements and costs associated with transmitting large amounts of data to a central location, contributing to overall cost efficiency.

Bandwidth optimization

In today's data-driven business environment, high-speed data processing is necessary, especially when dealing with large data volumes generated by numerous devices and applications. However, sending vast amounts of data to a centralized cloud for processing often leads to bandwidth issues, resulting in higher latency and potential service disruptions. These limitations could significantly hamper real-time analytics, remote operations, and user experience.

Here's where the edge computing capabilities of Microsoft Azure come into play, mitigating these limitations and risks. These edge computing solutions, such as Azure IoT Edge and Azure Stack Edge, process data closer to its source, significantly reducing the data volume that needs to travel across the network. This localized processing alleviates bandwidth strain and reduces latency, providing an optimized data flow.

Additionally, Azure edge solutions come with built-in data stream analytics, allowing for immediate insights and responses without needing back-and-forth communication with a central cloud. By mitigating bandwidth constraints and enhancing real-time data processing, the edge computing capabilities of Azure empower your organization to drive innovation, enhance user experience, and achieve operational efficiency, irrespective of the scale or location of your operations.

Enhanced security

In an increasingly digital world, securing sensitive data has become paramount for businesses across all sectors. Edge computing provides an additional layer of security that can significantly enhance an organization's data protection strategy. By processing and storing data closer to its source, edge computing reduces the volume of data traversing the network, minimizing exposure to potential cyber threats. This localized data processing and storage also enables businesses to maintain strict control over sensitive data, ensuring it doesn't leave a specific region or device if regulatory or business requirements dictate so. This can be particularly crucial for industries with stringent data sovereignty regulations, such as healthcare or finance. Furthermore, leading-edge computing solutions such as Azure Edge incorporate advanced security features, including encryption, anomaly detection, and secure device provisioning, providing robust defenses against potential cyber-attacks. Thus, by embracing edge computing, businesses can improve data security, maintain regulatory compliance, and reduce the risk of data breaches, ensuring they can confidently navigate the digital landscape.

Distributed computing

In the era of ubiquitous digital connectivity and massive data generation, using distributed computing through edge technology has become an appealing proposition for many business decision-makers. Distributed edge computing allows for dividing data processing tasks across a network of interconnected edge devices, effectively decentralizing data processing from a single central server to multiple edge locations. This approach offers several key advantages. Firstly, it significantly reduces latency by allowing data to be processed closer to the source, which is crucial for time-sensitive applications such as autonomous vehicles or remote surgery. Secondly, it optimizes bandwidth usage, reducing the amount of data transmitted across the network and mitigating congestion. Lastly, it enhances resilience by distributing the processing workload across multiple devices, mitigating the risk of a single point of failure. For instance, Azure Edge Zones supports distributed computing by bringing Azure services and applications to the network's edge, providing a seamless and reliable computing experience, irrespective of geographical distance or connectivity. As a result, organizations can facilitate real-time decision-making, improve operational efficiency, and make space for innovative opportunities by using distributed edge computing. Furthermore, by understanding the use cases and technical considerations for hybrid cloud, multicloud, and edge computing, they can make informed choices about strategically implementing and optimizing their hybrid cloud environment to meet their unique needs and objectives.

Looking at efficiency, reliability, security, and compliance

After exploring the various use cases and technical considerations for implementing hybrid, multicloud, and edge computing strategies in Azure, it is crucial to delve deeper into the aspects that significantly impact the success of these workloads and architectures. As we move forward in this section, we will focus on the critical factors of efficiency, reliability, security, and compliance. These elements play a vital role in ensuring that your organization can make the most of the potential of Azure while maintaining a robust and compliant infrastructure. Addressing these concerns can optimize your workloads and architecture, driving your organization's growth and digital transformation journey.

Efficiency – scaling and network performance

In the dynamic world of IT, business decision-makers are consistently tasked with delivering high performance, meeting the increasing demands of their users, and maintaining cost efficiency. This necessitates understanding scaling and network performance in the context of hybrid, multicloud, and edge computing environments:

Hybrid cloud: Regarding hybrid environments, Azure Stack ensures seamless scaling. But it also optimizes network performance by allowing you to run latency-sensitive applications on-premises while using sythe Azure public cloud for other tasks. By doing so, you maintain peak performance by reducing the network latency that can arise from remote data processing. In addition, the Azure ExpressRoute service optimizes network performance by establishing a private, high-speed connection between Azure and your on-premises data center, ensuring reliable and speedy data transfer.

Multicloud: With a multicloud strategy, Azure allows you to balance your workloads across different cloud providers, which can prevent network congestion and improve overall performance. You can use the rich toolset and capabilities of Azure in harmony with the services of other cloud vendors. Azure Virtual WAN is a boon in such settings, optimizing inter-network connectivity and ensuring the best path selection across multiple clouds, resulting in enhanced network performance.

Edge computing: Edge computing solutions, such as Azure IoT Edge and Azure Stack Edge, offer a strategic advantage for handling high-volume data produced at the network's edge. This approach enables efficient scaling across numerous edge devices and significantly reduces network latency by processing data near its source. As a result, you can achieve real-time data analysis and decision-making. Moreover, edge computing reduces the strain on network bandwidth by minimizing the amount of data that needs to be sent back to a central server, ensuring optimized network performance even as you scale.

In summary, understanding and optimizing for efficiency in terms of scaling and network performance is vital to realizing the full potential of hybrid, multicloud, and edge computing architectures. By making full use of the comprehensive suite of services and tools in Azure, business decision-makers can ensure that their IT infrastructure meets current business demands and is future-proof; able to scale seamlessly and maintain high-performance levels under varying workloads. These capabilities, coupled with the emphasis on interoperability and user-centric design built into Azure, empower organizations to navigate the complex landscape of cloud computing with agility and confidence, ultimately driving growth and innovation in an increasingly digital and connected business environment.

Reliability, high availability, disaster recovery, and backup

As we look at reliability concerning hybrid, multicloud, and edge computing, we emphasize high availability, disaster recovery, and backup strategies. Using the robust suite of services and tools Azure provides, business decision-makers can construct an IT infrastructure that not only is resilient but also ensures data integrity and application uptime, even in the face of unforeseen circumstances or disruptions.

Hybrid cloud: Azure Site Recovery provides a disaster recovery solution in a hybrid cloud environment, protecting major IT systems while ensuring compliance with various regulations. With automated replication of your workloads, Azure Site Recovery allows you to maintain business continuity even during a disaster. For backups, Azure Backup integrates with your on-premises systems and protects your data by orchestrating backups to Azure. Regarding high availability, Azure Load Balancer and Application Gateway help distribute traffic evenly to maintain application performance and availability during periods of high demand.

Multicloud: A multicloud strategy provides inherent high availability by distributing workloads across multiple cloud providers, reducing the risk of a single point of failure. Azure offers a suite of services for disaster recovery and backup in a multicloud environment. Azure Backup and Site Recovery can be used across multiple clouds, ensuring your data and applications are protected and can be restored promptly after an incident. This cross-cloud protection brings additional layers of resiliency to your multicloud strategy.

Edge computing: In edge computing scenarios, Azure IoT Edge and Azure Stack Edge bring cloud capabilities to the edge of your network. For high availability, these services can be deployed in multiple instances across edge locations, ensuring continuous operation even if one edge device fails. Azure also enables streamlined backup and disaster recovery for edge locations. With Azure Backup, you can manage edge device backups from the central Azure portal, and Azure Site Recovery extends disaster recovery capabilities to edge deployments.

In summary, when used effectively, hybrid, multicloud, and edge computing architectures can dramatically increase the reliability of your organization's IT infrastructure. Azure provides diverse solutions tailored to ensure high availability, enabling effective disaster recovery and securing backup options. When employed strategically, these capabilities protect against data loss and service disruptions, safeguarding your organization's operational continuity. However, it's essential to remember that achieving reliability is not a one-time effort but a continual evaluation, improvement, and adaptation process in response to evolving business needs and technology advancements. As such, your journey towards greater reliability with Azure is integral to your organization's larger digital transformation strategy.

Security – Zero Trust and defense in depth

Security solutions can't fix all issues; organizations need a holistic approach. We'll outline key defense-in-depth concepts and security technologies to support this strategy and apply them to Azure services.

The Zero Trust model emphasizes continual trust validation, not assumption. As users, networks, and devices operate beyond organizational control, trust must be based on verifiable claims.

Defense in depth employs multiple mechanisms to delay an attack, with each layer providing protection against breaches. For example, Microsoft uses this strategy across its data centers and Azure services, focusing on **Confidentiality, Integrity, and Availability (CIA)**.

Visualize defense in depth as layers securing data at the center. Each layer adds protection, slows attacks, and provides alerts:

1. **Data**: Ensure proper security for stored data, complying with regulations.
2. **Applications**: Prioritize secure, vulnerability-free applications and secure storage of sensitive data.
3. **Compute**: Secure VM access, implement endpoint protection, and keep systems updated.
4. **Networking**: Limit resource communication, restrict inbound/outbound access, and implement secure connectivity to on-premises networks.
5. **Perimeter**: Use DDoS protection, perimeter firewalls, and network attack identification.
6. **Identity and access**: Control infrastructure access, implement single sign-on and multifactor authentication, and audit events.
7. **Physical security**: Establish building security and control data center access.

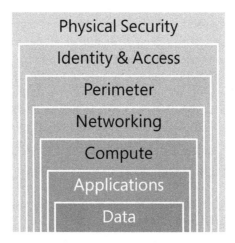

Figure 2.1: Defense-in-depth layers

As we delve into security, it's crucial to recognize that the nature of threats in today's digital world calls for a paradigm shift in our approach. Furthermore, hybrid, multicloud, and edge computing architectures inherently extend the security perimeter, thereby demanding a robust and comprehensive security strategy. In this context, Microsoft Azure Zero Trust and defense in depth frameworks offer compelling solutions to fortify your IT infrastructure.

Hybrid cloud: Hybrid cloud environments, which combine on-premises infrastructure with public cloud services, require comprehensive security strategies. Zero Trust in this context means not automatically trusting any requests, regardless of whether they originate internally or externally. Azure **Active Directory** (**AD**), Azure Policy, and Microsoft Defender for Cloud enforce Zero Trust principles across your hybrid cloud by authenticating and authorizing every request based on identity, location, and other attributes. Defense in depth is also essential, and Azure provides layers of protection with network security, data encryption, access controls, and threat detection and response capabilities.

Multicloud: In a multicloud strategy, where workloads are distributed across multiple cloud providers, Zero Trust and defense in depth principles are just as applicable. Azure provides tools such as Azure Arc, which extends Azure services and management to other clouds, thus enabling consistent policy enforcement, identity management, and threat protection across your multicloud environment. This cross-cloud approach ensures that Zero Trust principles and layered defenses are maintained, regardless of where your workloads run.

Edge computing: In edge computing scenarios, where data processing occurs closer to data sources, security challenges can be unique. Zero Trust principles imply that every edge device and data source must be authenticated and authorized. Azure IoT Edge and Azure Stack Edge provide the capabilities to implement Zero Trust at the edge, with features for secure device provisioning, encrypted communications, and automatic updates. Defense in depth at the edge involves securing devices, connections, and data. Azure provides end-to-end security with hardware-level protections, secure network connectivity, and encryption for data at rest and in transit.

In summary, embracing Azure Zero Trust and defense-in-depth strategies is paramount to ensuring the security of your hybrid, multicloud, and edge computing architectures. These principles provide a holistic, layered approach to security, from the data center to the user and everywhere in between. Furthermore, they encapsulate the contemporary understanding of the ever-evolving threat landscape, incorporating a dynamic and adaptable model rooted in continuous verification and multilayered protection. Hence, a robust security strategy that adheres to these principles is indispensable in pursuing digital transformation and innovation, safeguarding your assets, and reinforcing trust in your business operations.

Compliance – regulatory standards and industry norms

Compliance with regulatory standards and industry norms is a pivotal factor that needs to be meticulously considered while formulating your Azure strategy for hybrid, multicloud, and edge computing. Operating within the bounds of compliance shields your organization from legal repercussions and reinforces trust with your customers, stakeholders, and partners.

Azure provides comprehensive tools and services to aid your organization's compliance journey. As the first primary cloud provider to adopt the ISO 27018 privacy standard, Azure is committed to robust security and privacy protections. In addition, Azure offers more than 90 compliance certifications, including GDPR, HIPAA, and FedRAMP, serving various industries, including healthcare, finance, and government. This extensive suite of certifications can significantly streamline your compliance operations.

Hybrid cloud environments: The hybrid capabilities built into Azure ensure data integrity and security on-premises and in the cloud. Azure Stack, for instance, extends Azure services and capabilities to your on-premises environment, enabling you to apply the same compliance controls across your hybrid infrastructure.

Multicloud strategy: While this approach uses best-of-breed services from different cloud providers, compliance can be a complex challenge. Azure addresses this by providing Azure Policy and Microsoft Defender for Cloud, which allows you to implement consistent policy enforcement and monitor the compliance status across multiple cloud providers.

Edge computing: Compliance risks can increase due to the widespread distribution of data processing and storage. Azure addresses these challenges by providing robust tools such as Azure IoT Edge and Azure Data Box Edge that ensure data is processed and stored securely at the edge while adhering to compliance regulations.

However, it is essential to remember that compliance is a shared responsibility. While Azure provides the tools and resources to achieve compliance, your organization must implement them effectively. This involves regularly reviewing your compliance posture, conducting audits, and making necessary adjustments to ensure that your hybrid, multicloud, and edge computing deployments remain compliant with the evolving regulatory landscape. Your compliance strategy should be an ongoing effort, integrated with your business processes, and fully supported by top management to ensure its effectiveness and longevity.

Microsoft Azure reference architectures

As we've explored the various aspects of efficiency, reliability, security, and compliance in the context of hybrid, multicloud, and edge computing, it's essential to consider how these principles can be applied in practice. The next step in our journey is to delve into Microsoft Azure reference architectures, which provide a solid foundation for designing and deploying optimized, secure, and compliant solutions. These reference architectures showcase best practices, proven patterns, and real-world examples to help you understand how to use Azure services in your organization effectively. By drawing upon these resources, you can ensure that your workloads and architecture in Azure are well-suited to meet your unique business requirements and challenges.

Browse Azure architectures in the following resource:

```
https://learn.microsoft.com/azure/architecture/browse/?products=azure
```

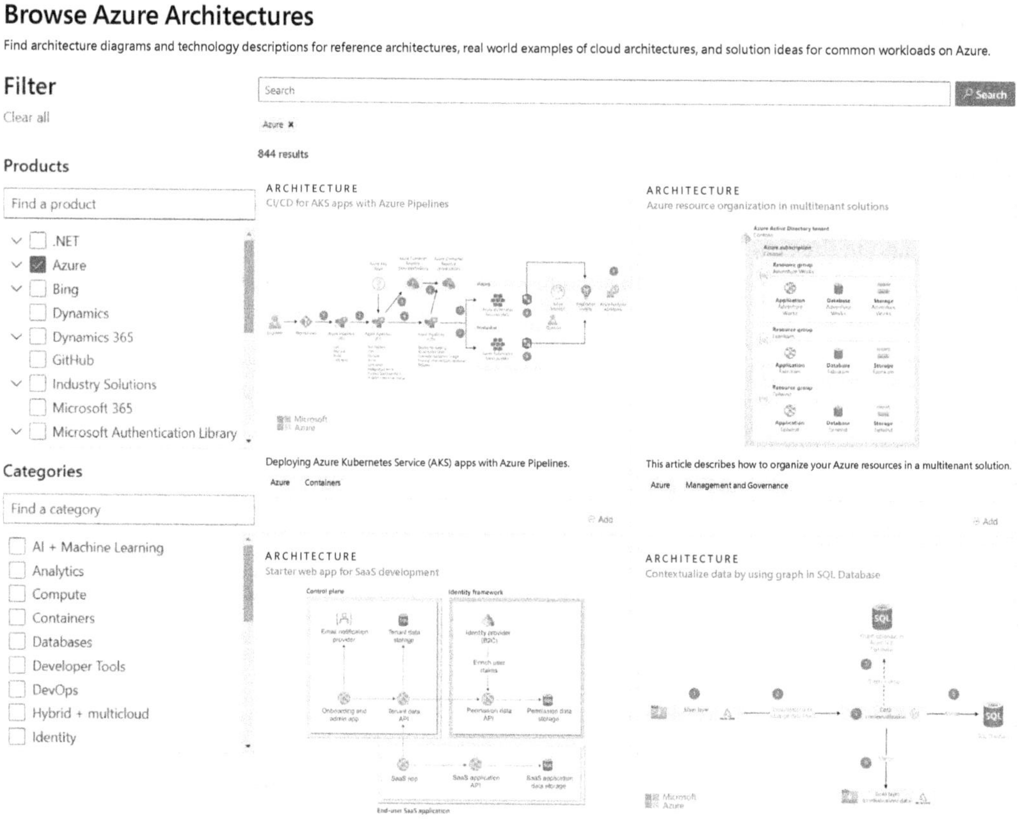

Figure 2.2: Azure reference architectures for different use cases

Important operational considerations

As we have discussed various aspects of workloads and architecture in Azure, including hybrid, multicloud, and edge computing strategies, we must focus on broader operational considerations. While technical factors play a significant role in the success of your workloads and architecture, ensuring seamless integration with your organization's operational processes and practices is equally vital. The upcoming section will delve into critical operational considerations affecting your Azure environment's management, monitoring, and maintenance. By addressing these aspects, you can build a comprehensive and well-rounded approach to optimizing your cloud infrastructure, aligning it with your organization's goals and objectives.

Moving just your resources to the cloud is taking advantage of only a tiny portion of what the cloud can bring to your organization. Along with the technical capabilities that the cloud delivers, you can improve your operational capabilities as well. From improving developer agility to improving the visibility of the health and performance of your application, you can use the cloud to enhance the operational capabilities of your organization.

Operational excellence means ensuring complete visibility of your application's performance across various environments and delivering the best possible user experience. It encompasses agile development and release practices, allowing your business to adapt quickly to changes. Enhanced operational capabilities lead to faster development and release cycles, ultimately benefiting your application's users.

Several principles can guide your pursuit of operational excellence through hybrid, multicloud, and edge computing architectures.

Design, build, and orchestrate with modern practices

Modern architectures should incorporate DevOps and continuous integration across on-premises, cloud, and edge environments. This approach enables you to automate deployments using **Infrastructure as Code** (**IaC**), automate application testing, and build new environments as needed. DevOps is a cultural and technical shift that can yield significant benefits for organizations that embrace it. By breaking down silos and fostering collaboration across all stages of a project, you can instill operational excellence in your organization.

Azure provides a comprehensive suite of tools and services that support modern design, build, and orchestration practices in hybrid, multicloud, and edge computing environments. With Azure, organizations can achieve operational excellence through improved agility, streamlined processes, and efficient resource management:

- **Infrastructure as Code** (**IaC**): Azure enables you to implement IaC using **Azure Resource Manager** (**ARM**) templates, Azure Bicep, and Terraform. These tools allow you to define, provision, and manage resources across hybrid and multicloud environments using code, promoting consistency, repeatability, and reducing manual intervention.

- **Continuous Integration and Continuous Deployment (CI/CD)**: Azure DevOps and GitHub Actions provide robust CI/CD pipelines, enabling seamless integration of code changes, automated testing, and rapid deployment of applications. By incorporating CI/CD into your development processes, you can accelerate releases and ensure a high level of application quality across various environments.

- **Containerization**: Azure supports containerization using **Azure Kubernetes Service (AKS)** and **Azure Container Instances (ACI)**. Containers enable you to package and deploy applications consistently across hybrid, multicloud, and edge environments. This approach simplifies deployment, scaling, and management while maintaining a high level of application performance and availability.

- **Serverless computing**: Azure Functions and Azure Logic Apps enable serverless computing, allowing you to build event-driven applications without worrying about infrastructure management. In addition, serverless computing promotes agility and cost-efficiency by automatically scaling resources based on demand and charging only for the computing time used.

- **Microservices architecture**: Azure Service Fabric and AKS support the development and deployment of microservices-based applications. Microservices enable you to break applications into smaller, independent components, increasing agility, scalability, and resilience across hybrid, multicloud, and edge environments.

- **Application monitoring and insights**: Azure Monitor, Application Insights, and Azure Log Analytics provide comprehensive monitoring, logging, and diagnostics capabilities. These tools help you gain insights into application performance, identify issues, and optimize resource usage across your hybrid, multicloud, and edge architectures.

By embracing these modern practices and utilizing the extensive toolset available to them in Azure, organizations can enhance operational excellence and drive innovation.

Utilize monitoring and analytics for operational insights

Implement comprehensive monitoring, logging, and instrumentation systems throughout your hybrid, multicloud, and edge architectures. Effective monitoring lets you detect issues before they impact users, identify performance problems, and uncover cost inefficiencies. A robust monitoring strategy is essential for optimizing application performance and reducing waste across diverse environments.

Monitoring and analytics are crucial in achieving operational excellence in hybrid, multicloud, and edge computing environments. Azure provides a comprehensive suite of monitoring and analytics services that can help organizations gain valuable insights, optimize resources, and maintain high application performance and reliability levels:

- **Azure Monitor**: A robust monitoring service that collects, analyzes, and acts on telemetry data from various Azure resources, including hybrid and multicloud environments. It provides a unified view of your infrastructure and applications, enabling you to detect and diagnose issues, optimize performance, and proactively manage resources.

- **Application Insights**: An **application performance management** (**APM**) service that helps you monitor, diagnose, and troubleshoot issues in your applications. It collects detailed information about application performance, exceptions, and user behavior, providing actionable insights to improve application stability, reliability, and user experience.

- **Azure Log Analytics**: A log management service that collects and analyzes log data from various sources, including applications, infrastructure, and network devices. It enables you to perform complex queries, correlate events, and visualize data to identify trends, anomalies, and potential issues across your hybrid, multicloud, and edge environments.

- **Azure Network Watcher**: A network monitoring and diagnostics service that helps you monitor network performance, diagnose connectivity issues, and ensure optimal network security. It provides tools such as Traffic Analytics, Connection Monitor, and IP Flow Verify to gain insights into network traffic patterns, performance metrics, and security risks.

- **Microsoft Defender for Cloud**: Defender for Cloud is a comprehensive security management and threat detection service that helps you protect your hybrid, multicloud, and edge environments. It provides continuous monitoring, threat intelligence, and security recommendations, enabling you to detect and respond to potential security threats proactively.

- **Azure Cost Management**: A financial management service that helps you monitor and optimize your cloud spending across Azure and other cloud providers. It provides insights into resource usage, cost trends, and budgeting, allowing you to optimize resource allocation and reduce overall cloud expenditure.

By utilizing the monitoring and analytics services in Azure, organizations can gain valuable operational insights, improve application performance, optimize resource usage, and maintain a high level of security and compliance.

Testing

Incorporate testing into your application deployment and ongoing operations across on-premises, cloud, and edge environments. A robust testing strategy helps detect issues before deployment and ensures proper communication between dependent services and your application. In addition, comprehensive testing can identify performance bottlenecks and potential security vulnerabilities in both preproduction and production environments, ultimately enhancing the user experience.

Effective testing is integral to operational excellence in hybrid, multicloud, and edge computing environments. By implementing a comprehensive testing strategy, organizations can identify and address issues before they impact users, ensuring high-quality and reliable applications. Azure provides a robust set of tools and services to support various types of testing, from unit testing to performance and security testing:

1. **Azure Test Plans**: Azure DevOps is a suite of services designed to streamline application development, testing, and deployment. It includes Azure Test Plans, a service that allows you to create, manage, and execute test cases and track and analyze test results. In addition, Azure Test Plans supports manual and automated testing, enabling you to validate your applications across different environments and configurations thoroughly.

2. **Azure Pipelines**: A part of Azure DevOps, this provides a powerful platform for implementing CI/CD. With Azure Pipelines, you can automate the build, test, and deployment process, ensuring that your applications are rigorously tested at every stage of the development lifecycle.

3. **Application performance and user experience**: Azure Monitor helps you collect, analyze, and act on telemetry data from your applications and infrastructure. With Application Insights, a feature of Azure Monitor, you can gain deep insights into your application's performance and user experience. This information enables you to identify bottlenecks, performance issues, and potential problems, helping you proactively address issues before they impact users.

4. **Load testing**: Azure provides various tools and services for load testing, which helps you assess your applications' performance, scalability, and reliability under heavy load. For example, you can use Azure DevOps or third-party tools integrated with Azure to simulate high levels of user traffic, analyze performance metrics, and identify areas for optimization.

5. **Security testing**: Ensuring the security of your applications is crucial in hybrid, multicloud, and edge environments. Microsoft Defender for Cloud provides a comprehensive set of tools and recommendations to help you protect your applications and data. Additionally, you can use Azure services such as Azure AD and Azure Key Vault to manage access control, authentication, and encryption.

6. **Container and microservices testing**: With the growing adoption of containerization and microservices, testing strategies must evolve to cover these new architectures. Azure supports containerized applications with services such as **Azure Kubernetes Service (AKS)** and Azure Container Instances. In addition, you can use Azure DevOps and other tools to build and test containerized applications, ensuring they run efficiently and securely across different environments.

By incorporating the testing capabilities of Azure into your operational processes, you can help ensure your applications' quality, performance, and security. This, in turn, leads to improved user experiences, increased agility, and better overall operational excellence.

Summary

Modernizing your organization with hybrid, multicloud, and edge computing in Azure can drive significant efficiency, agility, and innovation improvements. We've explored the fundamental concepts of hybrid, multicloud, and edge computing and their unique advantages, use cases, and technical considerations. By embracing unified operations and aligning your strategy with your business needs, you can create new opportunities and stay ahead of the competition.

This chapter also discussed the importance of operational excellence, strategic considerations, and best practices for workload and architecture management. Azure provides a comprehensive suite of tools and services to help you address challenges such as data storage, application development, compliance, and cost optimization. By examining the reference architectures in Azure and following the guidance provided, you can ensure a successful transition to a modern, flexible, and secure infrastructure.

As a technical decision maker, it's essential to recognize the immense potential of hybrid, multicloud, and edge computing in Azure and capitalize on these technologies to drive your organization forward. In addition, by focusing on efficiency, reliability, security, and compliance, you can empower your business to thrive in today's fast-paced, ever-changing landscape.

Migration and Modernization

In today's fast-paced business environment, companies must innovate constantly to stay ahead of their competition. Innovation is vital to endure the competitive business climate and meet customers' growing demands. Cloud computing is one of the most prominent modern technological advancements that enables businesses to achieve their innovation goals.

As the technology landscape rapidly evolves, it is becoming increasingly important for businesses to migrate to the cloud and modernize their IT infrastructure. The benefits of cloud migration and modernization are numerous, including increased agility, scalability, and cost savings. Microsoft Azure is one of the leading cloud providers, offering a wide range of services and solutions to help businesses migrate and modernize their IT infrastructure.

In this chapter, we will cover the following topics:

- Stages of migration and modernization
- Frameworks for cloud adoption
- How to maximize cloud investment

Benefits of modernization and migration to the cloud

The benefits of cloud migration and modernization are proven to be plentiful. In this section, we will discuss the following key benefits of migration and modernization:

- **Increased agility**: One of the key benefits of cloud computing is increased agility. With the cloud, businesses can quickly and easily spin up new resources as needed without significant upfront investment. This flexibility allows companies to experiment with new ideas and products, free from the concern of potential failure.

  For example, consider a startup that wants to test a new product. By utilizing the cloud, the startup can spin up a new environment in a matter of minutes, test its product, and easily pivot if necessary. This agility allows startups to move quickly, innovate, and stay ahead of the competition.

- **Improved collaboration**: Teamwork is essential for fostering innovation, and the cloud plays a pivotal role in facilitating collaboration. Through cloud migration and modernization, businesses can securely provide their employees with unified access to resources and data, regardless of their geographical location. This shared access to resources helps teams to collaborate more effectively and encourages the generation of fresh ideas.

  For example, a company can use a cloud-based collaboration platform to bring together teams from several departments or even across different geographical locations. This platform can facilitate real-time collaboration, enabling teams to seamlessly work together on projects in a highly efficient and synchronized manner.

- **Access to advanced tools and technologies**: Another way that cloud migration and modernization can drive innovation is by providing access to advanced tools and technologies that might be too expensive or complex to implement on-premises. Cloud providers invest heavily in developing new tools and services, and by migrating to the cloud, businesses can use these innovations without the need for significant upfront investment.

  As an example, a company can accelerate its development of a more accurate prediction model by consuming existing machine learning algorithms that are readily available on a cloud platform. The ability to access advanced tooling available on the cloud can help businesses stay ahead of the curve and drive innovation in their industry.

- **Improved scalability**: The scalability of cloud computing can help businesses innovate by enabling them to scale their operations quickly and easily. As businesses grow, the ability to quickly scale operations to meet evolving demands becomes critical. Cloud computing simplifies this process, providing businesses with a smooth and efficient means of scaling their operations.

  A company, for instance, might experience a sudden spike in website traffic due to the launch of a viral marketing campaign. By leveraging the scalability of the cloud, the company can quickly spin up additional resources to handle the increased traffic, ensuring that their website remains responsive and that they do not miss out on potential customers. When the campaign concludes, the company can scale down the resources, optimizing cost efficiency without compromising on performance.

- **Cost savings**: Cost savings are one of the most significant advantages of cloud computing, and these savings can be reinvested in innovation. By migrating to the cloud, businesses can reduce their capital expenditures and shift to an operational expenditure model. This shift can free up funds that can be used to drive innovation.

  For example, a company that migrates to the cloud can reduce its hardware and software expenses, as well as the costs associated with maintaining and upgrading these systems. These cost savings can be used to fund research and development activities, allowing the company to innovate and stay ahead of the competition.

- **Improved security**: Security is a critical concern for businesses, especially when it comes to innovation. The cloud can help businesses improve their security posture, enabling them to innovate with greater confidence.

  Cloud providers invest heavily in security, and by migrating to the cloud, businesses are protected by this investment. Furthermore, companies can take advantage of advanced security features, such as encryption, access controls, and network segmentation, which can help protect against data breaches and other security threats.

In the next section, we will explain why many organizations have chosen Azure as their migration and modernization destination.

Reasons for choosing Azure

Microsoft Azure is one of the leading cloud providers, offering a variety of services and solutions to help businesses migrate and modernize their IT infrastructure. Many organizations have chosen Azure as their migration and modernization destination due to the following reasons:

- **Scalability**: Azure provides a scalable cloud infrastructure that can easily grow or shrink based on your needs. This can help you reduce costs by only paying for the resources you use.

- **Flexibility**: Azure supports a wide range of programming languages, operating systems, and frameworks, which makes it easy to deploy and manage applications.

- **Security**: Azure provides a secure cloud infrastructure that is compliant with industry standards and regulations. It also includes built-in security features, such as encryption and multifactor authentication, to protect your data and applications.

- **Cost-effectiveness**: Azure offers a pay-as-you-go pricing model, which means you only pay for the resources you use. This can help you reduce your infrastructure costs and improve your overall ROI.

- **Integration**: Azure integrates with an extensive range of Microsoft and third-party tools and services, making it easy to connect applications and data to other systems.

Ultimately, the decision to migrate or modernize with Azure depends on an organization's specific business needs and goals. With the benefits of and reasons for migration and modernization to Azure fully explained, we are ready to plan for your first migration and modernization project.

In the next section, we will take a look at the three stages of migration and modernization.

The three stages of migration and modernization

The three stages of migration and modernization (see *Figure 3.1*), namely planning, implementation, and operations, form a comprehensive framework for organizations transitioning their workloads to Azure.

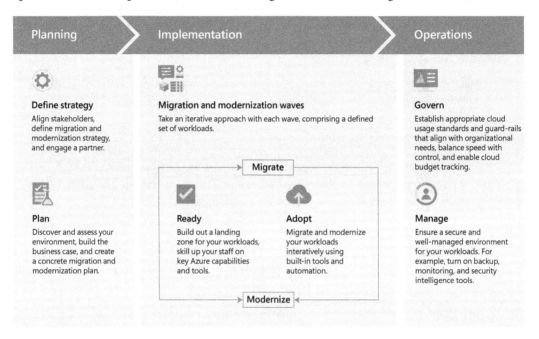

Figure 3.1: Three stages of migration and modernization

We will provide a comprehensive overview of each of these stages in the following sections.

1. Planning stage

Planning for migration and modernization to the cloud is an essential step that can save considerable time and effort, and reduce overall costs. Before embarking on a migration and modernization journey, it is important to develop a comprehensive plan. This plan should include an assessment of your current IT infrastructure, a detailed migration strategy, and a plan for post-migration optimization and management. The assessment should identify any potential roadblocks and provide a clear understanding of the scope and complexity of the migration.

In this section, we will discuss some essential planning steps to consider when migrating to Azure.

Define your strategy

1. **Define your migration and modernization goals and objectives**: Before you start any migration and modernization, it is essential to define your goals and objectives. These steps will help you determine what you want to achieve with the migration and modernization, which applications and data to move, and what the expected outcomes are. Document these business outcomes.

2. **Involve and align key stakeholders**: To ensure a smooth and efficient migration process that aligns with organizational goals, it is beneficial to enlist broad support across the organization. This can be achieved by establishing a center of excellence consisting of a cross-functional team comprising IT, finance, and business owners.

3. **Engage a cloud migration and modernization partner**: To enhance your cloud skillset and mitigate risks during the migration and modernization of your workloads, it is advantageous to collaborate with a **managed service provider** (**MSP**). By partnering with an MSP that offers comprehensive support throughout the entire process and beyond, organizations can tap into their expertise and experience in managing cloud environments. This collaboration not only assists in navigating the complexities of migration but also ensures ongoing support and guidance in optimizing and maintaining your cloud infrastructure. With an MSP as a trusted partner, organizations can effectively augment their cloud capabilities, reduce risk, and achieve successful outcomes in their cloud initiatives.

Plan for your move

1. **Assess your current environment**: To plan for a successful migration and modernization, you need to understand the strengths and limitations of your current environment. This assessment will help you identify what can be migrated as is, what needs to be modified, and what cannot be migrated. You can gain valuable insights into your dependencies using automated cloud migration tools. These tools enable you to efficiently plan inventory for your infrastructure and assess your on-premises environments. By using these tools, you can receive guidance on right-sizing your resources, obtain workload-level cost estimates, and access performance metrics.

2. **Make a business case for migration and modernization**: Determine the potential cost savings associated with migrating to Azure by conducting a thorough evaluation of your **total cost of ownership** (**TCO**). This entails calculating and comparing the TCO of Azure with that of a comparable on-premises deployment. By performing this analysis, you can gain insights into the financial advantages of migrating to Azure, enabling you to make informed decisions and identify potential cost-saving opportunities. We have a full section on maximizing the value of your cloud investment later in this chapter.

3. **Build a holistic plan**: Choosing the proper migration strategy is critical to ensuring a successful migration and modernization project. There are several migration and modernization strategies to choose from, depending on your goals, application requirements, workload priorities, timelines, milestones, resources, and funding. Be sure to get buy-in from leadership and your new migration center of excellence. Some common strategies include the following:

    - **Rehosting**: This involves moving applications and data to Azure without making significant changes to the application's architecture. This is part of migration.

    - **Refactoring**: This involves making significant changes to the application's architecture and code to take advantage of Azure services and capabilities. This is part of modernization.

    - **Rebuilding**: This involves rebuilding the application from scratch on Azure using cloud-native services and architectures. This is part of modernization.

    - **Retiring**: This involves retiring applications that are no longer needed. By retiring obsolete or unused applications, organizations can reinvest the savings to cultivate new business initiatives.

2. Implementation stage

During the implementation stage, the focus is on transferring workloads, data, and infrastructure to Azure. To facilitate a structured and organized migration process, it is recommended to build landing zones as a foundational framework. This involves creating a well-architected environment that aligns with best practices, security measures, and governance standards. Once the landing zones are established, organizations can proceed with migrating and modernizing their workloads in waves, ensuring a controlled and manageable transition to Azure. This approach allows for incremental migrations, minimizing disruptions and optimizing the overall migration process.

2.1. Get ready for the move

1. **Build cloud skills**: Ensure your IT and app development teams are well versed in cloud technologies, migration tools, and operational processes. By making an upfront investment in training, you enable your teams to quickly adapt to the demands of cloud adoption and facilitate the scaling of your migration efforts with greater efficiency. This proactive approach equips your organization with the necessary expertise to navigate the complexities of the cloud, positioning you for success in achieving your migration goals and optimizing your cloud environment for maximum value.

2. **Set up landing zone for your workloads**: Mitigate potential governance issues during and after migration by adhering to landing zone best practices. Utilizing preconfigured landing zones that incorporate networking, identity management, security, and governance elements helps strike a balance between agility and adherence to organizational standards. Organizations can follow these best practices to ensure that their cloud environment is set up with proper governance controls, reducing the risk of compliance and security breaches. This approach provides a solid foundation for managing and maintaining governance during the migration process and beyond, enabling organizations to navigate cloud adoption with confidence and peace of mind.

3. **Review best practices for Azure readiness**: To ensure the proper configuration of your existing and future landing zones, it is essential to expand and validate any modifications using Azure readiness best practices. By following these guidelines, organizations can verify that their landing zones adhere to recommended standards and are optimized for performance, security, and governance. This proactive approach helps mitigate potential risks and ensures that the landing zones are well prepared to support current and future workloads effectively. By aligning with Azure readiness best practices, organizations can confidently deploy and manage their landing zones, setting the stage for a successful cloud environment.

2.2. Migrate your workloads

1. **Make cloud migration easier with Azure Migrate**: Simplify the process of discovering, assessing, and migrating your workloads by using Azure Migrate. Azure Migrate is a centralized hub for all your migration automation requirements. It provides you with the necessary tools and guidance to seamlessly execute your migration. From a central dashboard, you can access a wide array of resources, track your progress, and stay updated on the status of your migration. We will talk more about Azure Migrate in the *Maximizing the value of your cloud investment* section.

2. **Assess, migrate, optimize, and promote workloads iteratively**: Use an iterative process of migrating one workload at a time or a small collection of workloads per release. This method ensures that each workload is thoroughly assessed, migrated, optimized, and promoted to meet production demands with each iteration. Organizations can effectively manage the migration process, mitigating risks and ensuring that workloads are adequately prepared for production environments. This iterative approach enables continuous improvement and fine-tuning, allowing organizations to optimize the performance, scalability, and reliability of their workloads in the cloud.

2.3. Modernize your apps and data

1. **Modernize iteratively at any stage**: The process of modernization encompasses activities such as refactoring, rearchitecting, or rebuilding your applications and data. Using modernization techniques allows organizations to derive various benefits, including enhanced app innovation, increased agility, and accelerated developer velocity. Modernization can be undertaken at any stage of the migration journey, whether it is before, during, or after migrating your workloads. This flexibility enables organizations to strategically modernize their applications and data, allowing the full potential of cloud technologies to drive business growth and success.

2. **Refactor apps and databases for speed and productivity**: When aiming to make minimal changes to your applications for seamless integration with Azure, consider refactoring or repackaging them. Refactoring involves making targeted modifications to ensure easy connectivity to Azure services. For instance, you can refactor relational databases by directly migrating them into a cloud-based database service such as Azure SQL Database. This approach allows you to take advantage of the benefits offered by Azure services while minimizing disruptions to your existing application architecture.

3. **Rearchitect apps and databases for cloud scalability and productivity**: Rearchitecting is the recommended approach when you want to modify and extend the functionality and code of your applications to optimize them for cloud scalability. This involves transforming monolithic applications into a set of interconnected microservices that can work together and scale effortlessly. By adopting a microservices architecture, organizations can enhance the agility and scalability of their applications, allowing for more efficient resource utilization and overall performance improvements in the cloud. Rearchitecting enables organizations to make use of the full potential of cloud technologies and take advantage of the scalability benefits provided by platforms such as Azure, resulting in improved flexibility, resilience, and the ability to meet evolving business demands.

4. **Rebuild with cloud-native technologies to accelerate developer velocity**: Rebuilding an application using Azure cloud solutions is a recommended approach when there is a need to recreate the app from scratch. This strategy is particularly useful when existing applications have limited functionality or a limited expected lifespan. By rebuilding the application using the cloud-native capabilities of Azure, organizations can take advantage of the full range of services and features offered by the platform. This approach allows for the creation of modern, scalable, and robust applications that are specifically designed to work with the capabilities of Azure. Rebuilding provides an opportunity to optimize the app's architecture, enhance its functionality, and extend its lifespan, ensuring long-term viability and alignment with the evolving requirements of the cloud environment.

3. Operations stage

Finally, in the operations stage, the organization focuses on governing, securing, and managing its cloud environments. With a robust set of tools and services available on Azure, organizations can establish comprehensive governance frameworks to ensure adherence to policies, compliance requirements, and regulatory standards. Additionally, Azure provides centralized monitoring and management capabilities, allowing organizations to gain deep insights into their cloud resources, optimize performance, and efficiently allocate costs.

3.1. Govern and secure your workloads

1. **Get visibility into and more control over your security posture**: Enhance your ability to detect and respond swiftly to threats across hybrid environments by using intelligent threat protection solutions such as Azure Security Center. This comprehensive security platform enables organizations to proactively identify and mitigate potential risks through advanced threat detection and response capabilities. Additionally, organizations can secure their entire infrastructure by utilizing cloud-native **security information and event management (SIEM)** solutions such as Azure Sentinel. Azure Sentinel provides centralized monitoring, advanced analytics, and automated responses to security incidents, empowering organizations to strengthen their overall security posture. These solutions enable organizations to effectively safeguard their environments, mitigate risks, and respond promptly to security threats.

2. **Build and scale your apps and workloads quickly while maintaining control**: Building on the foundation of your landing zone, it is important to establish and maintain a balanced combination of standard and custom policies to effectively govern your cloud subscriptions and resources while ensuring compliance. By utilizing Azure policy management capabilities, organizations can define and enforce a set of rules and guidelines that align with their specific regulatory requirements and internal governance standards. These policies help maintain consistency, security, and compliance across the cloud environment, ensuring that resources are provisioned and used in accordance with established guidelines.

3.2. Manage and cost-optimize your cloud environments

1. **Become familiar with the tools, offers, and guidance from Azure**: Achieve greater operational efficiency and control cloud expenditures by closely monitoring and adjusting your cloud spending taking advantage of exclusive offers available in Azure. One cost-saving tip is using reserved instance discounts, allowing you to commit to specific Azure resources in advance and receive significant cost reductions. Another way to optimize your budget is by reusing your existing on-premises licenses in Azure to maximize the value of your software investments. By actively managing and optimizing your cloud spending through these strategies, organizations can effectively drive operational efficiency, reduce costs, and make the most of their Azure resources.

2. **Simplify management**: You can efficiently manage your workloads across multiple environments with solutions such as Azure Arc. With Azure Arc, you gain centralized control and visibility over your workloads, allowing you to effectively monitor their performance, analyze real-time insights, and identify trends. Furthermore, safeguarding your workloads is extremely important, and Azure provides reliable cloud backup and disaster recovery solutions to help ensure the continuity and protection of your critical data and applications. Organizations can streamline workload management, proactively address performance issues, and enhance the resilience and security of their workloads across diverse environments by leveraging these tools and services.

In summary, careful planning can help ensure a successful migration to Azure. By following these best practices, organizations can minimize risks, reduce costs, and optimize their migration endeavors.

Microsoft Azure offers a comprehensive suite of products and solutions to help businesses migrate and modernize their IT infrastructure.

In the next section, we will explore two frameworks that offer organizations valuable guidance and resources to navigate the complexities of cloud migration and ensure a smooth transition to the cloud environment.

Two versatile frameworks for cloud adoption

The Microsoft Cloud Adoption Framework and Microsoft Azure Well-Architected Framework are two versatile frameworks offered by Microsoft to assist organizations in their transition to the cloud and enhance the efficiency of their cloud-based solutions.

The Microsoft Cloud Adoption Framework is a comprehensive guide that outlines best practices, methodologies, and strategies for successful cloud adoption. It offers a structured approach to planning, implementing, and governing cloud initiatives, ensuring organizations can maximize the benefits of cloud technologies while managing risks and challenges effectively.

On the other hand, the Microsoft Azure Well-Architected Framework is a set of guiding principles, best practices, and architectural patterns specifically designed for building secure, high-performing, resilient, and efficient cloud-based solutions on the Azure platform. It provides a systematic methodology to evaluate workloads against these pillars, identify potential areas of improvement, and implement the recommended architectural best practices.

Together, the Cloud Adoption Framework and Azure Well-Architected Framework provide organizations with the tools they need to accelerate their cloud adoption, optimize their cloud solutions, and achieve long-term success in the ever-evolving world of cloud computing. Let's explore each of these frameworks in detail.

Microsoft Cloud Adoption Framework

The Microsoft Cloud Adoption Framework provides holistic best practices, guidelines, and tools for organizations looking to adopt cloud technologies. This full lifecycle framework can help organizations assess their cloud readiness, develop a cloud adoption strategy, and implement a cloud governance model. The reference architectures, templates, and tools can be used to guide organizations through each stage of the cloud adoption process. This framework emphasizes continuous improvement and optimization by providing ongoing guidance and feedback to help organizations progressively optimize their cloud environments.

The Microsoft Cloud Adoption Framework consists of the following methodologies, each with its own set of best practices and guidelines:

Strategy	Define business objectives, assess the current state, and develop a cloud adoption strategy that aligns with the goals and requirements of the organization. `https://learn.microsoft.com/azure/cloud-adoption-framework/strategy/`
Plan	Create a detailed actionable implementation plan that includes tasks, timelines, and resource requirements, and identifies potential risks and mitigations. `https://learn.microsoft.com/azure/cloud-adoption-framework/plan/`
Ready	To get ready for cloud adoption, create a landing zone to host the workloads that you plan to build in or migrate to the cloud. `https://learn.microsoft.com/azure/cloud-adoption-framework/ready/`

Adopt	The Adopt methodology provides guidance on migrating, modernizing, innovating, and relocating workloads in Azure. These four processes align to different phases in the cloud adoption journey. Each phase has distinct goals, solutions, and benefits. `https://learn.microsoft.com/azure/cloud-adoption-framework/adopt/`
Manage	Manage operations for cloud and hybrid solutions. `https://learn.microsoft.com/azure/cloud-adoption-framework/manage/`
Govern	Govern your environment and workloads in an iterative process. `https://learn.microsoft.com/azure/cloud-adoption-framework/govern/`
Secure	Cloud security is an ongoing journey of incremental progress and maturity, not a static destination. `https://learn.microsoft.com/azure/cloud-adoption-framework/secure/`
Organize	Align the teams and roles supporting your organization's cloud adoption efforts. Prepare the organization's people, processes, and technology for cloud adoption by establishing governance policies, defining roles and responsibilities, and building the necessary skills and capabilities. `https://learn.microsoft.com/azure/cloud-adoption-framework/organize/`

The Cloud Adoption Framework is designed to help organizations maximize the value of their cloud investment by providing a structured approach to cloud adoption. The framework provides a set of best practices and tools to help organizations minimize risks, reduce costs, and optimize the value of their cloud investments. By using the Cloud Adoption Framework, organizations can ensure that their cloud adoption journey is well planned, structured, and aligned with business goals and objectives.

To learn more about the Microsoft Cloud Adoption Framework, please visit `https://learn.microsoft.com/azure/cloud-adoption-framework/overview`.

Microsoft Azure Well-Architected Framework

The Microsoft Azure Well-Architected Framework provides a collection of best practices, guidelines, and principles that enable the design and operation of reliable, secure, efficient, and cost-effective systems in the cloud.

Figure 3.2: Five pillars of architectural excellence

The framework consists of five pillars of architectural excellence (see *Figure 2*):

1. **Reliability**: This pillar focuses on ensuring application availability and resilience by designing for fault tolerance, implementing backup and disaster recovery strategies, and testing for failure.

2. **Cost Optimization**: This pillar focuses on optimizing costs without sacrificing performance by identifying cost drivers, minimizing waste, and using the pricing models and tools Azure provides.

3. **Operational Excellence**: This pillar focuses on improving operational processes and practices by establishing monitoring and logging strategies, automating tasks, and implementing best practices for managing incidents and changes in production.

4. **Performance Efficiency**: This pillar focuses on optimizing application performance by designing for scalability, selecting appropriate compute and storage resources, and leveraging caching and content delivery networks.

5. **Security**: This pillar focuses on protecting data and applications from unauthorized access and threats by implementing security controls, encrypting data, and managing identities and access.

By following the Azure Well-Architected Framework, organizations can ensure that their workloads are designed and deployed according to industry best practices. This can help organizations optimize their cloud resources for cost and performance and reduce the risk of security breaches.

To learn more about the Microsoft Azure Well-Architected Framework, please visit `https://learn.microsoft.com/azure/well-architected/`.

In the next section, we will explore tools that can help organizations maximize the value of their cloud investment.

Maximizing the value of your cloud investment

As more and more organizations move their workloads to the cloud, it is essential to maximize the value of their cloud investments. Microsoft Azure offers many tools and frameworks that can help organizations optimize their cloud usage, reduce costs, and improve performance.

Microsoft Cost Management and Azure Advisor

Microsoft Cost Management and Azure Advisor are two tools that can help organizations monitor and optimize their cloud costs.

Microsoft Cost Management

Cost Management provides a range of tools and services to help organizations track and analyze their cloud costs, including cost breakdowns by resource, cost alerts, and budgeting and forecasting tools.

To learn more about Microsoft Cost Management, please visit `https://learn.microsoft.com/azure/cost-management-billing/cost-management-billing-overview`.

Azure Advisor

Azure Advisor is a tool that provides recommendations for optimizing cloud usage based on best practices and historical usage patterns. It gives recommendations for cost optimization, security, performance, and availability.

To learn more about Azure Advisor, please visit `https://learn.microsoft.com/azure/advisor/advisor-overview`.

By using Cost Management and Azure Advisor, organizations can monitor their cloud usage and identify opportunities to optimize their cloud resources for cost and performance.

Azure savings opportunities

Azure offers a range of savings opportunities that can help organizations reduce their cloud costs. These include the following:

- **Reserved VM Instances**: Reserved VM Instances allow organizations to commit to using specific compute resources for a one- to three-year term, which can result in significant cost savings compared to on-demand pricing.

- **Spot VM Instances**: Spot VM Instances allow organizations to make the most of spare compute capacity in Azure data centers at a discounted price. This can be a cost-effective way to run non-critical workloads.

- **Hybrid Benefit**: Hybrid Benefit allows organizations with Software Assurance to use their existing Windows Server and SQL Server licenses in Azure, which can result in significant cost savings.

- **Azure Cost Management**: Azure Cost Management provides a range of tools and services to help organizations monitor and optimize their cloud costs. This includes cost tracking and analysis, budgeting and forecasting, and recommendations for cost optimization.

By taking advantage of these savings opportunities, organizations can reduce their cloud costs and maximize the value of their cloud investment.

To learn more about Azure savings opportunities, please visit `https://learn.microsoft.com/azure/cost-management-billing/savings-plan/`.

Additional tools for maximizing your cloud investment

In addition to the tools mentioned previously, Azure also offers several essential tools that play a vital role in streaming migration, establishing a robust cloud foundation, and enabling cost-effective resource management.

Azure Migrate

One of the first steps in maximizing the value of your cloud investment is to ensure that you have a comprehensive understanding of your existing infrastructure. Azure Migrate is a tool that can help you assess your on-premises infrastructure, including physical servers, virtual machines, and databases, and give recommendations for migration to Azure.

Azure Migrate provides a centralized hub for migration projects, including the discovery, assessment, and migration phases. It can help you assess the readiness of your workloads for migration and offer guidance on the right Azure resources to use for migration. By using Azure Migrate, you can reduce the risk of downtime and data loss during migration and optimize your cloud resources for performance and cost. This all-in-one solution streamlines your migration journey, making it easier to plan, execute, and monitor the successful transition of your workloads to Azure.

To learn more about Azure Migrate, please visit `https://learn.microsoft.com/azure/migrate/migrate-services-overview`.

Azure landing zones

An Azure landing zone is a pre-built environment that delivers a foundation for deploying workloads in Azure. It includes a set of best practices and guidelines for deploying workloads in Azure, together with security, networking, and governance.

By using an Azure landing zone, organizations can accelerate their cloud adoption and ensure that their workloads are deployed according to best practices. This can help organizations optimize their cloud resources for cost and performance and reduce the risk of security breaches.

To learn more about Azure landing zones, please visit `https://learn.microsoft.com/azure/cloud-adoption-framework/ready/landing-zone/`.

Cost calculators

One of the biggest benefits of cloud computing is the ability to scale resources up and down as needed, which can help reduce costs. However, it is essential to have a clear understanding of your cloud costs to ensure that you are getting the most value for your investment. The following cost calculators can help you with this:

- **Azure Pricing calculator**: The Azure Pricing calculator can help you estimate the cost of running your workloads in Azure: `https://azure.microsoft.com/pricing/calculator/`

- **Azure Total Cost of Ownership (TCO) calculator**: The Azure TCO calculator can help you understand the cost savings of running workloads in Azure compared to on-premises infrastructure: `https://azure.microsoft.com/pricing/tco/calculator/`

By using cost calculators, you can make informed decisions about your cloud usage and optimize your cloud resources for cost and performance.

In summary, maximizing the value of your cloud investment requires a comprehensive understanding of your cloud usage and a structured approach to cloud adoption and governance. Azure offers a range of tools and frameworks that can help organizations optimize their cloud usage, reduce costs, and improve performance. By using tools such as Azure Migrate, cost calculators, the Cloud Adoption Framework, savings opportunities, Azure landing zones, the Well-Architected Framework, Cost Management, and Azure Advisor, organizations can ensure that they are making informed decisions about cloud usage and optimizing their cloud resources for cost and performance.

In the next section, we will explore some workload migration scenarios.

Workload migration scenarios

Workload migration is the process of moving an application or system from one environment to another. In the context of cloud computing, workload migration typically refers to moving an application or system from an on-premises environment to the cloud. This can include a range of scenarios, such as rehosting to Azure Virtual Machines, application migration, data migration, and hybrid migration.

Rehosting to Azure Virtual Machines

Rehosting involves moving an existing workload to the cloud without making any changes to the application or system. This approach is sometimes referred to as "lift and shift," as it involves lifting the application or system from its current environment and shifting it to the cloud.

Azure Virtual Machines is a service that allows organizations to create and run virtual machines in the cloud. By rehosting on Azure Virtual Machines, organizations can benefit from the scalability and flexibility of the cloud while maintaining the same application or system architecture and configuration.

To learn more about Azure Virtual Machines, please visit `https://learn.microsoft.com/azure/virtual-machines/overview`.

Application migration

Application migration involves moving an application from one environment to another while making some changes to the application itself. This can include changes to the application architecture or configuration and the underlying infrastructure.

Azure provides a range of tools and services to support application migration, including Azure App Service, Azure Kubernetes Service, and Azure Service Fabric. These services allow organizations to run applications in the cloud using modern deployment and scaling patterns, such as containerization and microservices.

Data migration

Data migration involves moving data from one environment to another. This can include moving databases, data warehouses, and other types of data storage.

Azure offers several services to support data migration, such as Azure Database Migration Service and Azure Data Factory. These services allow organizations to migrate data from on-premises environments or other cloud providers to Azure, while minimizing downtime and ensuring data integrity.

Hybrid migration

Hybrid migration involves moving some workloads to the cloud while keeping other workloads on-premises. This approach can be useful for organizations that want to take advantage of the scalability and flexibility of the cloud while maintaining certain workloads on-premises for regulatory or other reasons.

Azure provides several services to support hybrid migration, such as Azure Stack and Azure Arc. These services allow organizations to run Azure services and manage workloads across on-premises, multicloud, and edge environments, providing a consistent experience across all environments.

In summary, workload migration is a critical aspect of cloud adoption, and there are several scenarios that organizations may encounter, including rehosting on Azure Virtual Machines, application migration, data migration, and hybrid migration. By using the tools and services provided by Azure, organizations can migrate workloads to the cloud while minimizing downtime, ensuring data integrity, and optimizing performance and cost.

In the upcoming section, we will learn the strategies for achieving cloud scalability and optimizing performance.

Achieving cloud scale and maximizing performance

Achieving cloud scale and maximizing performance are critical aspects of cloud adoption. Organizations need to ensure that their cloud resources can handle high traffic and performance demands while maintaining cost efficiency.

In this section, we will discuss how Azure can help organizations achieve cloud scale and maximize performance through features such as Azure autoscaling and considerations for compute and storage performance.

Azure autoscaling

Azure autoscaling is a feature that allows organizations to automatically scale their cloud resources up or down based on changing workload demands. Autoscaling helps organizations maintain optimal performance and reduce costs by ensuring that they have adequate resources to meet demand at all times.

Azure autoscaling supports both horizontal and vertical scaling. Horizontal scaling involves adding or removing instances of an application or workload, while vertical scaling involves increasing or decreasing the size of a single instance. Autoscaling can be triggered based on a range of metrics, including CPU usage, network traffic, and queue length.

To learn more about Azure autoscaling, please visit `https://learn.microsoft.com/azure/architecture/best-practices/auto-scaling`.

Compute and storage performance considerations

When designing and deploying workloads in the cloud, organizations need to consider compute and storage performance to ensure that their applications and systems can handle high traffic demands.

Some key considerations include the following:

- Choosing the appropriate virtual machine size based on workload requirements, such as CPU and memory requirements, and expected traffic demands.

- Using Azure Storage performance tiers to optimize performance and cost for different types of workloads. For example, Azure Premium Storage provides high-performance storage for I/O-intensive workloads, while Azure Blob Storage provides cost-effective storage for large amounts of unstructured data.

- Using caching technologies, such as Azure Cache for Redis, to improve application performance by reducing the need to retrieve data from disk.

- Leveraging Azure **Content Delivery Network** (**CDN**) to improve the performance of web applications by caching static content closer to employees and reducing latency.

- By considering compute and storage performance, organizations can ensure that their workloads are optimized for high traffic demands while maintaining cost efficiency.

In summary, achieving cloud scale and maximizing performance are critical aspects of cloud adoption. Azure provides several features and considerations to help organizations achieve these goals, including Azure autoscaling, choosing the appropriate virtual machine size, leveraging Azure Storage performance tiers, using caching technologies, and using Azure CDN. Organizations can ensure that their workloads are optimized for high traffic demands while maintaining cost efficiency by following best practices for compute and storage performance.

In the next section, we will explore the topic of enterprise-grade backup and disaster recovery on Azure.

Enterprise-grade backup and disaster recovery on Azure

In today's digital world, data is the lifeblood of any business. As a result, backup and disaster recovery are essential for maintaining business continuity and avoiding data loss. With Azure, Microsoft offers enterprise-grade backup and disaster recovery solutions that are reliable, scalable, and cost-effective. We will explore two of these solutions: Azure Backup and Azure Site Recovery.

Azure Backup

Azure Backup is a simple and cost-effective backup solution that allows you to protect your data in the cloud. With Azure Backup, you can back up data from on-premises and cloud environments, including virtual machines, SQL Server, and files and folders. Azure Backup is highly scalable, allowing you to back up hundreds of terabytes of data.

One of the key benefits of Azure Backup is its ability to provide backup and retention policies that meet compliance requirements. You can set up policies for long-term retention and archival, and Azure Backup has built-in encryption to protect your data in transit and at rest.

To get started with Azure Backup, you need to create a backup vault. A backup vault is a container that holds your backups and gives a centralized management experience for your backup policies. You can create a backup vault using the Azure portal or Azure PowerShell. Once you have created a backup vault, you can configure backup policies for your workloads.

To learn more about Azure Backup, please visit https://learn.microsoft.com/azure/backup/backup-overview.

Azure Site Recovery

Azure Site Recovery is a disaster recovery solution that allows you to replicate your on-premises virtual machines to the cloud. In the event of a disaster, you can fail over to the replicated virtual machines in Azure, ensuring business continuity.

With Azure Site Recovery, you can replicate virtual machines from VMware vSphere or Microsoft Hyper-V environments to Azure. Azure Site Recovery provides continuous replication, ensuring that your virtual machines are always up to date in the event of a failover.

One of the key benefits of Azure Site Recovery is its ability to provide site-to-site failovers. This means that you can replicate your virtual machines to a secondary site, and if your primary site goes down, you can fail over to the secondary site, ensuring business continuity.

To get started with Azure Site Recovery, you need to create a Recovery Services vault. A Recovery Services vault is a container that holds your resources and gives a centralized management experience for your disaster recovery policies. You can create a Recovery Services vault using the Azure portal or Azure PowerShell. Once you have created a Recovery Services vault, you can configure disaster recovery policies for your virtual machines.

To learn more about Azure Site Recovery, please visit `https://learn.microsoft.com/azure/site-recovery/site-recovery-overview`.

In summary, backup and disaster recovery are critical components of any business continuity plan. With Azure Backup and Azure Site Recovery, Microsoft offers enterprise-grade solutions that are reliable, scalable, and cost-effective. By leveraging these solutions, you can protect your data, ensure business continuity, and meet compliance requirements.

Azure migration and modernization best practices and support

When it comes to migrating and modernizing workloads to Azure, there are several best practices and support options available to ensure a smooth and successful migration.

Here are some Azure migration and modernization best practices:

1. **Assess your workloads**: Before migrating, it is important to assess your current workloads and applications to determine which ones are suitable for migration to Azure. You can use Azure Migrate to assess your environment and identify any dependencies, as well as estimate costs and right-size resources.

2. **Choose the right migration and modernization strategy**: As we discussed earlier in this chapter, there are several migration and modernization strategies to choose from, including rehosting, refactoring, rebuilding, and retiring. Choose the strategy that best suits your business needs and goals.

3. **Optimize your environment**: Optimize your workloads for the cloud by leveraging Azure services including Azure SQL Database, Azure App Service, and Azure Cosmos DB. This will help improve performance and reduce costs.

4. **Ensure security and compliance**: Make sure to implement security best practices and ensure compliance with industry standards and regulations, such as HIPAA and GDPR.

5. **Train your team**: Ensure that your team has the necessary skills and training to manage and operate your new Azure environment. This includes training on Azure tools and services, as well as best practices for security and compliance.

In addition to these best practices, Azure offers a range of support options to help organizations migrate and modernize to the cloud:

1. **The official Azure documentation**: The Azure documentation provides a wealth of information on various migration scenarios, including lift-and-shift, modernization, and hybrid cloud deployments. It covers best practices for planning, executing, and optimizing your migration, as well as how to make the best use of Azure services and tools for each scenario.

    `https://learn.microsoft.com/azure/`

2. **Azure Migration and Modernization Program (AMMP)**: The AMMP is a comprehensive program that helps customers migrate their workloads to Azure with confidence. It offers a range of services, such as discovery and assessment, migration planning and execution, and post-migration optimization. AMMP also offers access to Azure experts, tools, and resources to help simplify and streamline the migration process.

   `https://www.microsoft.com/azure/partners/ammp`

3. **Azure Architecture Center**: The Azure Architecture Center provides guidance and resources on best practices for designing, deploying, and operating applications on Azure. It includes guidance on modernizing legacy applications, building cloud-native applications, and leveraging various Azure services and tools to optimize performance, security, scalability, and availability.

   `https://learn.microsoft.com/azure/architecture/`

4. **Azure App Service**: Azure App Service is a fully managed platform for building, deploying, and scaling web applications and APIs. It has a range of features and tools to simplify the migration process, including built-in support for popular languages and frameworks, automated deployment options, and seamless integration with Azure services such as Azure SQL Database and Azure Active Directory.

   `https://learn.microsoft.com/azure/app-service/overview`

5. **Azure SQL Database**: Azure SQL Database is a fully managed, intelligent database service that provides high availability, scalability, and security for your applications. It offers built-in migration tools and support for popular database engines, as well as advanced features such as intelligent performance tuning, automatic backups, and disaster recovery options.

   `https://learn.microsoft.com/azure/azure-sql/database/`

6. **Recommendations from Azure Advisor**: Azure Advisor is a free service that provides personalized recommendations for optimizing your Azure resources and services. It offers migration-specific recommendations such as right-sizing your virtual machines, optimizing storage usage, and using Azure services such as Azure Site Recovery and Azure Backup for disaster recovery and backup.

   `https://learn.microsoft.com/azure/advisor/advisor-overview`

7. **Free training with Microsoft Learn**: Microsoft Learn is a free, interactive learning platform that offers a range of training courses and resources on Azure migration and modernization. It includes hands-on labs, interactive exercises, and guided learning paths to help you gain the skills and knowledge needed to successfully migrate your workloads to Azure.

   `https://learn.microsoft.com/training/`

This chapter provided you with a comprehensive guide to migration and modernization. We wish you the best of luck with your migration and modernization journey!

Summary

Migration and modernization to the cloud can foster innovation within an organization. By leveraging the cloud's benefits, including increased agility, improved collaboration, access to advanced tools and technologies, improved scalability, cost savings, and improved security, businesses can stay ahead of the curve and drive innovation in their industry.

Cloud computing enables businesses to experiment with innovative ideas and products quickly, collaborate more effectively, access advanced tools and technologies, and scale their operations as needed. These benefits, combined with cost savings and improved security, make the cloud a powerful tool for innovation.

As businesses face increasing pressure to innovate and stay ahead of the competition, migration to and modernization on the cloud can provide the agility, scalability, and access to advanced tools and technologies needed to succeed in today's fast-paced business environment.

Azure offers a range of tools and resources to help you migrate your workloads to the cloud with confidence. By following best practices, using the right Azure services and tools, and taking advantage of the support options available, organizations can accelerate their cloud adoption journey and achieve their business objectives more efficiently.

In the next chapter, we will look at security in Azure.

Maximizing Azure Security Benefits for Your Organization

In today's business world, data has become one of the most valuable assets for any organization. Protecting that data is a top priority. **Identity and access management (IAM)** solutions are essential for ensuring the security and privacy of an organization's data. IAM solutions provide a framework for managing access to resources, applications, and data while ensuring that the identities of those accessing resources are secure and properly managed.

This chapter will discuss the Azure security benefits for organizations, including IAM, best practices for securing workloads on Azure, and the ability to deploy security solutions from the cloud to the edge using hybrid solutions.

To further enhance security, we will discuss how Microsoft Sentinel provides intelligent security analytics and threat intelligence across an enterprise by searching, analyzing, and visualizing data. Furthermore, we will review how organizations can also use Sentinel to correlate threat signals from various Microsoft 365 security services and Sentinel itself.

We will also review how the Microsoft cloud security benchmark provides security recommendations to secure workloads on Azure and how Microsoft Defender for Cloud enables visibility, detection, and responses to threats across multiple cloud platforms. To prevent advanced targeted attacks, we will see how Microsoft Defender for Identity detects suspicious user and device activity and how Microsoft Defender for Endpoint prevents, detects, investigates, and responds to advanced threats across devices. Finally, we will discuss how Microsoft Defender for Cloud Apps enables visibility and control of cloud usage to protect sensitive data and comply with regulatory requirements.

In this chapter, we will cover the following topics:

- Identity and access management
- Security features in Azure
- Securing Kubernetes clusters in Azure

Identity and access management

The importance of IAM solutions has grown significantly in recent years, particularly since organizations have switched to remote work. With more employees accessing company resources from outside the office, it has become more critical than ever to have robust IAM solutions in place. IAM solutions ensure that only authorized users have access to the right resources and are secured against unauthorized access or cyberattacks.

With IAM, organizations have the opportunity to improve how resources are managed and accessed by different types of users. These users could be employees, contractors, business partners, or customers with different access requirements. IAM solutions help organizations manage these different user types by providing **role-based access control** (**RBAC**) and other features that allow administrators to manage access levels and permissions.

Azure IAM solutions are the preferred choice for organizations as they provide scalable solutions for IAM. Azure IAM solutions provide the flexibility required as organizations grow and evolve. This scalability ensures that the IAM solution can effectively manage the increasing number of users and resources while maintaining security and regulatory compliance. IAM is a pivotal part of the security mechanisms necessary for organizations to manage their data and resources. Here are some benefits of implementing Azure IAM solutions within your organization:

- **Enhanced security**: These mechanisms are instrumental in protecting sensitive data and resources from unauthorized access, theft, and other security threats.

- **Regulatory compliance**: Industries are obligated to comply with data privacy regulations such as GDPR, HIPAA, and PCI DSS. IAM mechanisms can ensure regulatory compliance.

- **Improved productivity**: IAM can boost productivity by reducing the time and effort needed to manage resource access, which prevents delays and bottlenecks caused by unauthorized access attempts.

- **Reduced risk of insider threats**: IAM mechanisms help limit access to authorized personnel only, thus reducing the risk of insider threats to sensitive data and resources.

- **Simplified audit trails**: IAM simplifies audit trails by keeping a clear record of who accessed specific data and resources and at what time.

IAM solutions are essential for any organization that wants to ensure the security and privacy of its data. It provides a framework for managing access to resources, applications, and data while ensuring that the identities of those accessing those resources are secure and properly managed. With Azure RBAC, single sign-on, reverse proxy, **multi-factor authentication** (**MFA**), password management, and compliance capabilities, Azure helps organizations manage the different types of users that need access to resources and ensure that those resources are secured against unauthorized access.

Security benefits of Azure

Azure helps protect data while it's in transit, at rest, or even when it's in use. With Azure, organizations can benefit from various security capabilities, such as the following:

- **Advanced threat protection**: Azure provides advanced threat protection to detect and prevent cyber-attacks. It uses machine learning algorithms to analyze threats and identify patterns in data to identify potential threats. Azure also has built-in threat intelligence, which provides real-time information about known threats and helps organizations to prevent possible attacks.

- **Encryption and data protection**: Azure provides robust encryption and data protection capabilities, which are essential for ensuring the confidentiality, integrity, and availability of sensitive data. It encrypts data in transit and at rest using industry-standard protocols such as TLS and AES, client-side encryption, and server-side encryption using SSL certificates and customer-managed keys. Azure also provides data backup and recovery services, ensuring critical data is always available, even during a disaster.

- **IAM**: Azure provides robust IAM capabilities, which are essential for controlling access to sensitive data and applications. It allows administrators to manage resource access based on user roles and offers multi-factor authentication to ensure only authorized users have access.

- **Compliance and regulatory support**: Azure complies with a wide range of industry standards and regulatory requirements, such as HIPAA, ISO, and GDPR. It provides built-in compliance reporting and auditing features, which are essential for demonstrating compliance with these standards and regulations.

- **Secure development practices**: Azure provides secure development practices to help developers build secure applications. It provides tools and services that help developers detect and fix security vulnerabilities early in development, ensuring that applications are protected from the ground up.

- **Global security**: Azure has a global security infrastructure, which ensures that data and applications are secure no matter where they are located. It has a range of data residency options, allowing organizations to choose where their data is stored, and it has a robust network of global data centers, which are designed to provide high levels of security and availability.

Security best practices for identity and access control in Azure

IAM is a critical component of any security strategy, and by following these best practices, you can ensure maximum security for your applications and data in Azure.

The following security best practices for IAM in Azure can benefit your organization in several ways:

- **Role-based access control (RBAC)**: RBAC is a built-in feature of Azure that allows you to manage access to resources based on user roles. With RBAC, you can define granular permissions for each role, ensuring that users have access only to the resources they need to perform their job functions. Following the principle of least privilege is essential, giving users the minimum permissions necessary to perform their job functions.

- **Multi-factor authentication (MFA)**: MFA is a security feature that requires users to provide two or more forms of authentication to access a resource. This can include something the user knows (such as a password) and something the user has (such as a token). Enabling MFA adds an extra layer of security, making it more difficult for attackers to compromise user accounts.

- **Azure Active Directory (Azure AD) Conditional Access**: Azure AD Conditional Access is a policy-based feature that allows you to define rules that determine when and how users can access Azure resources. You can use it to enforce MFA, restrict access based on network location, and more. Azure AD Conditional Access can help you implement a Zero Trust security model, where users must be authenticated and authorized before accessing any resource.

- **Monitor and Audit**: Monitoring and auditing are critical to maintaining the security of your Azure environment. Azure provides several built-in monitoring and auditing tools that can help you to detect and respond to security incidents. Azure AD logs all user activities, providing detailed information about who accessed what resource and when. Azure Security Center provides a centralized view of security alerts, allowing you to respond to potential security threats quickly.

In addition to the preceding best practices, you can find a comprehensive overview of Azure security recommendations and patterns here: `https://learn.microsoft.com/azure/security/fundamentals/best-practices-and-patterns`. The following section will discuss how Microsoft Sentinel, a comprehensive security solution, can deliver intelligent security analytics and threat intelligence across an enterprise.

Delivering intelligent security analytics and threat intelligence using Microsoft Sentinel

Microsoft Sentinel, a unified **security operations (SecOps)** platform, focuses primarily on two fronts: **security information and event management (SIEM)** and **security orchestration, automation, and response (SOAR)**.

Microsoft Sentinel allows data collection across an organization and detects threats while minimizing false positives using Microsoft's analytics and threat intelligence solutions. Organizations can investigate threats, hunt for suspicious activities, and accelerate the response to incidents using the built-in orchestration and automation components available in Sentinel.

Through Sentinel, organizations can protect their critical assets by gaining visibility of security data and performing searches across all their data, including archive logs, investigating historical data, and then transforming data by enriching and filtering it as needed. Microsoft Sentinel provides the right tools for all members of a security team.

> **Note**
> Microsoft Sentinel is built on top of the Azure Monitor Log Analytics platform, a tool you can use through the Azure portal to edit and run log queries from data collected by Azure Monitor logs and interactively analyze results.

Log Analytics is a tool in the Azure portal that's designed to store and analyze massive amounts of data. Using **Kusto Query Language** (**KQL**), a specific language to join data from multiple tables, aggregate large sets of data, and perform complex operations, security operation professionals and researchers can quickly analyze, investigate, and remediate incidents using automated tools.

Let's take a look at the four main stages of Microsoft Sentinel:

Figure 4.1: Main focus areas Microsoft Sentinel

1. **Collecting data**: Like other SIEM solutions, Microsoft Sentinel collects data from devices, users, applications, on-premises, and multiple cloud providers. Once Microsoft Sentinel is enabled, organizations can use built-in or third-party `connectors` to collect data.

    In the case of physical servers and virtual machines, the Log Analytics agent can be installed, collect the logs, and forward them to Microsoft Sentinel. Organizations can also use Linux Syslog servers, install the Log Analytics agent, and forward the logs to Microsoft Sentinel.

2. **Detecting threats**: Microsoft Sentinel includes analytics capabilities that can detect potential threats and reduce false positives and vulnerabilities across an organization. Security analysts can benefit from this feature and perform complex investigations faster.

    Microsoft Sentinel Analytics helps detect, investigate, and remediate potential threats. Analytics rules and queries can be configured to detect issues and analyze data from various sources, such as servers, firewalls, sensors, networking devices, and identity correlations and anomalies.

    Analytic rules are a key concept of Microsoft Sentinel. Analytical rules can be added as queries that contain specific logic to discover threats and anomalous behaviors in an environment. While Microsoft provides built-in analytics rules and detections, organizations can always customize their analytics rules.

3. **Investigating anomalies**: Proactive security analysts handle security threats and translate data into meaningful events. This requires standardizing the processes and lists of tasks to investigate and remediate an incident.

    Since Microsoft Sentinel uses Log Analytics for query execution, security teams can search for long periods in large datasets using a search job on any type of log. Teams can also restore data to perform queries.

    Microsoft Sentinel also provides a compelling dashboard for handling incidents, including powerful search and query tools to hunt for threats across the organization's data sources. Once you connect data sources to your Microsoft Sentinel solution, you can investigate incidents, and each incident is created based on the analytics rules you configure. Think of an incident as an aggregation of relevant evidence for a specific investigation, including single or multiple alerts.

    Consider a scenario where a security analyst is performing a hunting operation or an investigation. Now, as these operations become more complex, the security analyst needs a way to simplify data analysis and visualizations.

    Microsoft Sentinel includes notebooks to help security analysts simplify how they work with the data, the code executed in the data, results, and visualizations of a specific investigation. So, if an investigation becomes too complex, notebooks can help you remember, view details of or save queries and the results of the investigation.

    Once the investigation is complete, it is time to use mechanisms to respond to security threats.

4. **Responding to incidents**: Microsoft Sentinel includes SOAR capabilities. One of the primary purposes of Sentinel is to automate any response and remediation tasks that are part of the responsibilities of a **Security Operations Center**.

    Therefore, you will find controls to help you manage incident handling and response automation, such as *automation rules* and *playbooks*.

    Automation rules are different from analytics rules. Automation rules help centrally manage the automation of incident handling, so when there's an incident, you can automate responses from multiple analytics rules, as well as tag, assign, and close incidents. Simply put, *automation rules* simplify workflows for a threat response orchestration process.

    On the other hand, think of *playbooks* as a collection of actions that can be executed in Sentinel as a routine. Playbooks contain a set of response and remediation actions and logic steps. You can run a playbook automatically or manually on demand, responding to alerts or incidents. Playbooks are based on workflows built in Azure Logic Apps.

Searching, analyzing, and visualizing data in Microsoft Sentinel

In this section, we will demonstrate how to configure Microsoft Sentinel. First, let's review the components we must configure before enabling Microsoft Sentinel.

Global prerequisites

To successfully enable Microsoft Sentinel, you need the following:

- An active Azure subscription
- A Log Analytics workspace
- A user with contributor role permissions where the Sentinel workspace resides

Let's begin.

Enabling Microsoft Sentinel using the Azure portal

Let's review how to enable Microsoft Sentinel using the Azure portal:

1. Go to the Azure portal and search for *Log Analytics*, as shown in *Figure 4.2*:

Figure 4.2 Log Analytics search

2. Provide the details to provision Log Analytics:

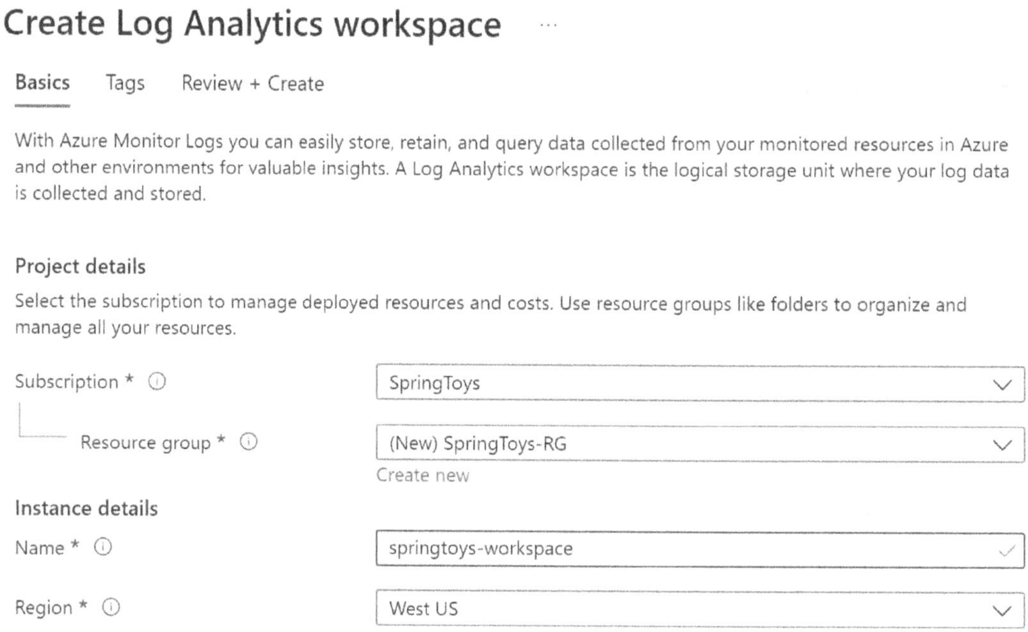

Create Log Analytics workspace   ...

Basics   Tags   Review + Create

With Azure Monitor Logs you can easily store, retain, and query data collected from your monitored resources in Azure and other environments for valuable insights. A Log Analytics workspace is the logical storage unit where your log data is collected and stored.

Project details

Select the subscription to manage deployed resources and costs. Use resource groups like folders to organize and manage all your resources.

Subscription * ⓘ | SpringToys   ⌄ |

 └─── Resource group * ⓘ | (New) SpringToys-RG   ⌄ |
                           Create new

Instance details

Name * ⓘ | springtoys-workspace   ✓ |

Region * ⓘ | West US   ⌄ |

Figure 4.3 Log Analytics workspace configuration

Next, we will enable Microsoft Sentinel.

3. Go to the top search bar of the Azure portal and look for *Sentinel*:

Figure 4.4 Microsoft Sentinel search

4. Now select the workspace we just created to enable Microsoft Sentinel:

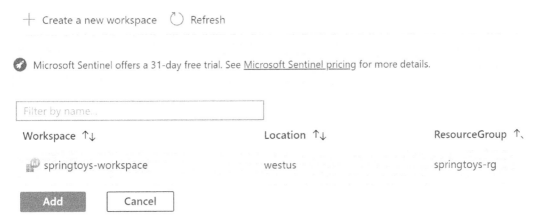

Figure 4.5 Microsoft Sentinel configuration

Up to 10 GB/day is free for both Microsoft Sentinel and Log Analytics during the trial period. The next step is to connect data sources to collect data in Microsoft Sentinel.

Setting up data connectors

Organizations can use data connectors to ingest data into Microsoft Sentinel. Some of these connectors are built-in connectors for Microsoft services, such as the Microsoft 365 Defender connector, which integrates data from different services, such as Azure AD, Office 365, Microsoft Defender for Identity, and Microsoft Defender for Cloud Apps.

Let's start by enabling the Microsoft 365 Defender connector.

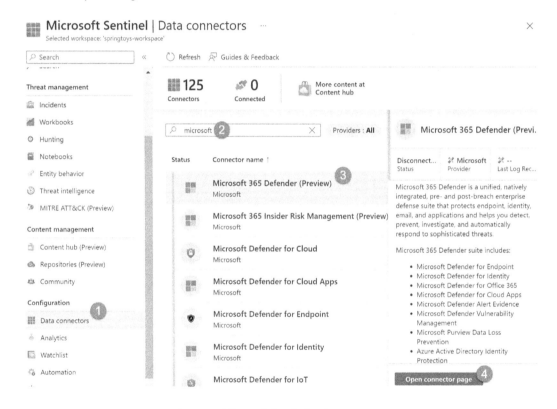

Figure 4.6 Microsoft 365 Defender connector

Once you open the connector page, you will see the log types that can be ingested in Microsoft Sentinel. The following figure shows the logs that can be ingested using the Microsoft 365 Defender connector:

Instructions   Next steps

Connect events

Connect logs from the following Microsoft 365 Defender products to Sentinel:

⌄   Microsoft Defender for Endpoint (0/10 connected) ⓘ

⌄   Microsoft Defender for Office 365 (0/5 connected)

⌄   Microsoft Defender for Cloud Apps (0/1 connected)

⌄   Microsoft Defender for Identity (0/3 connected)

⌄   Microsoft Defender Alert Evidence (0/1 connected)

⌄   Microsoft Defender Vulnerability Management - Coming soon!

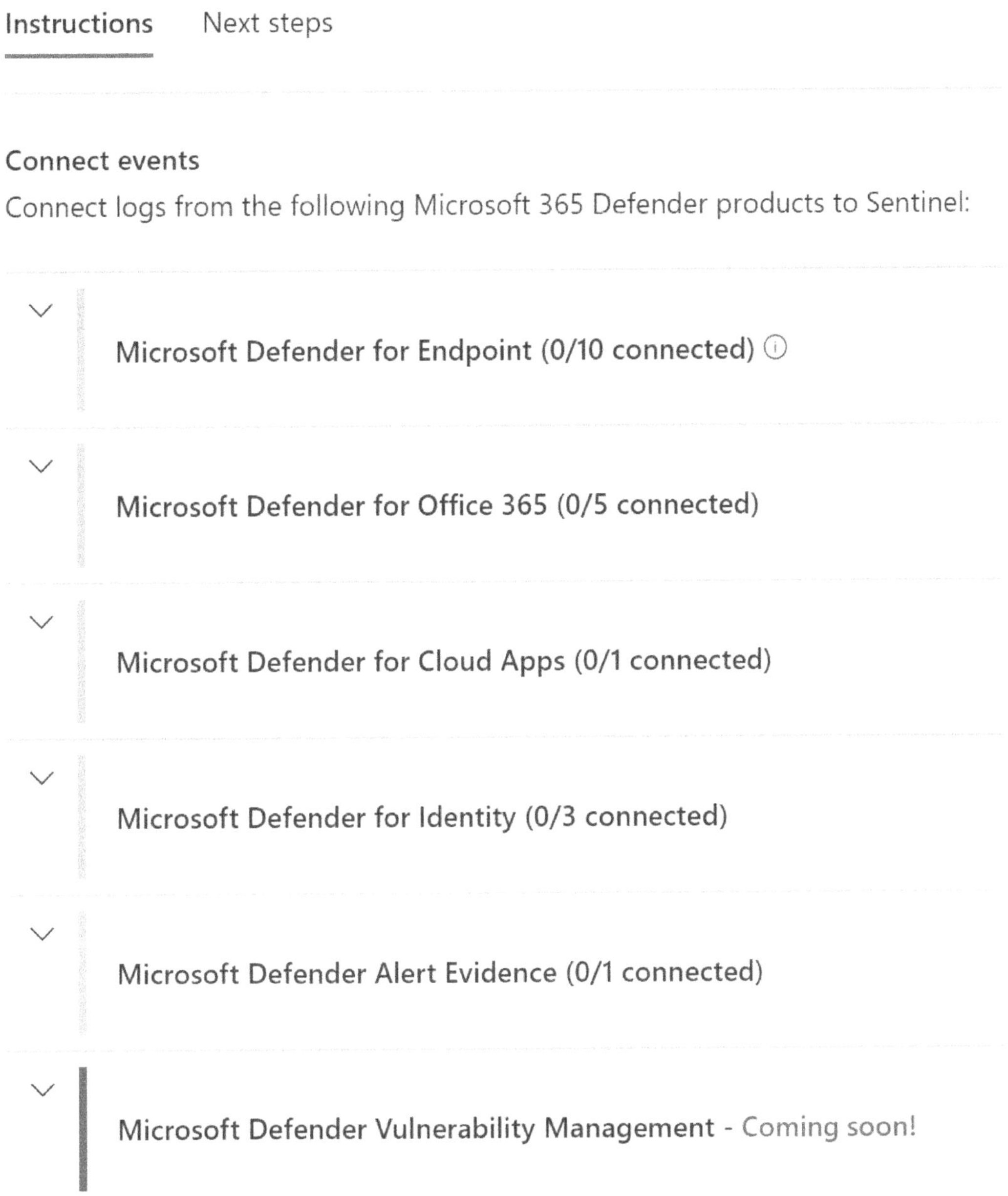

Figure 4.7 Microsoft 365 Defender connector

You can select the specific log event you want to collect for each product. For example, if we choose Microsoft Defender for Endpoint and expand the options, you will see the particular event types, as shown here:

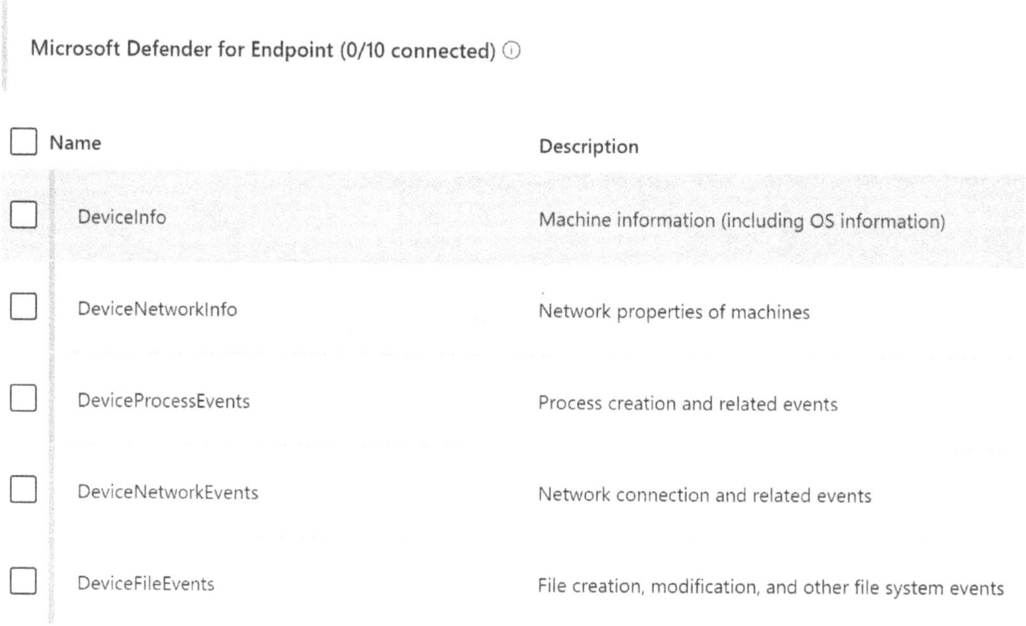

Microsoft Defender for Endpoint (0/10 connected) ⓘ

Name	Description
DeviceInfo	Machine information (including OS information)
DeviceNetworkInfo	Network properties of machines
DeviceProcessEvents	Process creation and related events
DeviceNetworkEvents	Network connection and related events
DeviceFileEvents	File creation, modification, and other file system events

Figure 4.8 Event types to collect

You can also review the workbooks and the built-in queries included in this connector, as shown here:

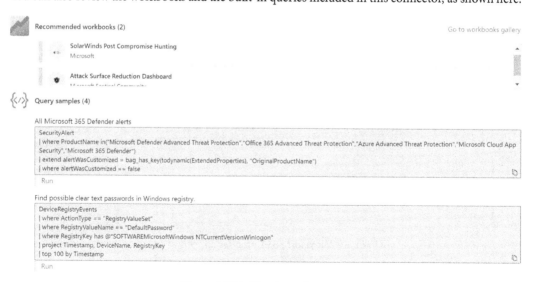

Figure 4.9 Workbooks and queries

In addition, the Microsoft 365 Defender connector also provides you with relevant analytics templates that you can use as needed:

Severity ↑↓	Name ↑↓	Rule type ↑↓	Data sources	Tactics	Techniques
High	Zinc Actor IOCs domains hashes IPs an...	Scheduled	DNS (Preview) +14 ⓘ	Persistence	T1546
High	Probable AdFind Recon Tool Usage	Scheduled	Microsoft 365 Defe...	Discovery	T1018
High	Dev-0530 IOC - July 2022	Scheduled	Cisco ASA +10 ⓘ	Impact	T1486
High	AV detections related to Zinc actors	Scheduled	Microsoft 365 Defe...	Impact	T1486
High	AV detections related to Ukraine threats	Scheduled	Microsoft 365 Defe...	Impact	T1485
High	KNOTWEED AV Detection	Scheduled	Microsoft 365... +1 ⓘ	Execution	T1203
High	Known ZINC Comebacker and Klackrin...	Scheduled	DNS (Preview) +12 ⓘ		T1071 +1 ⓘ
High	Prestige ransomware IOCs Oct 2022	Scheduled	Microsoft 365... +1 ⓘ	Execution	T1203
High	DEV-0270 New User Creation	Scheduled	Security Event... +1 ⓘ	Persistence	T1098
High	Hive Ransomware IOC - July 2022	Scheduled	Cisco ASA +3 ⓘ	Impact	T1486
High	Solorigate Network Beacon	Scheduled	DNS (Preview) +8 ⓘ	Command and ...	T1102
High	NOBELIUM IOCs related to FoggyWeb ...	Scheduled	F5 Networks +11 ⓘ	Collection	T1005

Relevant analytics templates (72)   Go to analytics templates

Figure 4.10 Analytics templates

So far, we have configured Microsoft Sentinel and the Microsoft 365 Defender data connector. Microsoft 365 Defender includes the following:

- Microsoft Defender for Endpoint
- Microsoft Defender for Identity
- Microsoft Defender for Office 365
- Microsoft Defender for Cloud Apps
- Microsoft Defender Alert Evidence
- Microsoft Defender Vulnerability Management
- Microsoft Purview Data Loss Prevention
- Azure Active Directory Identity Protection

Once you have enabled Microsoft Sentinel and connected data sources to ingest data and use them for analysis, the next step is to secure your workloads.

The following section will review how organizations can tailor their security controls to their specific needs while adhering to industry-standard security practices by using the Microsoft cloud security benchmark.

Securing your workloads using the Microsoft cloud security benchmark

Securing your workloads is crucial in today's digital landscape, and the Microsoft cloud security benchmark provides organizations with a comprehensive set of guidelines and best practices to ensure maximum security. Based on its extensive experience with cloud-based solutions, Microsoft has created this benchmark to provide organizations with a framework for implementing security controls and monitoring solutions.

The Microsoft cloud security benchmark is a framework created by Microsoft to help organizations secure their workloads on the Azure cloud platform. It covers various security topics, such as IAM, network security, data protection, and compliance. The benchmark provides a flexible and adaptable approach to security controls, enabling organizations to tailor their security controls to their specific needs while following industry-standard security practices.

Using the Microsoft cloud security benchmark can benefit organizations significantly as it provides a structured and standardized approach to security. The benchmark is organized into different levels of security controls, making it easy for organizations to identify the specific security controls they need to implement to secure their workloads. It also provides clear guidance on implementing each security control, including best practices, recommended configurations, and step-by-step instructions. This helps to ensure that organizations can implement the necessary security controls effectively and efficiently.

The Microsoft cloud security benchmark also provides guidance on how to assess the effectiveness of security controls and how to address any identified gaps or vulnerabilities. Microsoft recommends that organizations use the security benchmark in conjunction with other security tools and services to achieve a comprehensive security posture. As it is based on Microsoft's extensive experience with cloud-based solutions, the Microsoft cloud security benchmark is scalable and is used by organizations to ensure that their workloads are secure and compliant with relevant regulations and standards.

The Microsoft cloud security benchmark includes two main components: security controls and service baselines. The security controls broadly apply across cloud workloads and identify the stakeholders involved in planning, approving, or implementing the recommendations. On the other hand, the service baselines apply the security controls to specific cloud services, providing tailored recommendations for their security configurations.

The Microsoft cloud security benchmark covers a range of control domains:

- Network security
- Identity management
- Privileged access
- Data protection
- Asset management
- Logging and threat detection
- Incident response
- Posture and vulnerability management
- Endpoint security
- Backup and recovery
- DevOps security
- Governance and strategy

Each domain includes specific recommendations for securing resources, such as establishing secure network connections, implementing IAM systems, protecting privileged access, ensuring data protection, managing assets, detecting and responding to threats, assessing security posture, securing endpoints, and establishing a security strategy and governance approach.

The Microsoft cloud security benchmark includes a list of recommendations for securing cloud services in a single or multi-cloud environment. A benchmark ID identifies each recommendation and corresponds to CIS Controls `v7.1`, `v8`, `PCI-DSS v3.2.1`, and `NIST SP 800-53 r4` controls.

The recommendation includes information on security principles, Azure and AWS guidance, implementation details, and additional context. Additionally, each recommendation identifies the customer security stakeholders who are accountable, responsible, or consulted for the respective control.

The Microsoft cloud security benchmark is available for free usage, and to ensure compliance with other standards, you can enable an appropriate Defender plan.

Steps to implement the Microsoft cloud security benchmark for securing Azure workloads

To get started with the Microsoft cloud security benchmark, your organization should ensure they have an Azure subscription and the necessary permissions to access and manage Azure resources.

Next, your organization should determine which workloads to assess and prioritize. The Microsoft cloud security benchmark covers a wide range of workloads, including virtual machines, containers, and Azure services.

The organization should identify which workloads are most critical to their business and focus on those first. They should then use the benchmark to assess the security of those workloads and identify any gaps or vulnerabilities.

Based on the results, your organization can develop a remediation plan and take action to improve its security posture. Continuous monitoring and periodic reassessment can help ensure ongoing compliance with the benchmark and maintain a high level of security for Azure workloads.

In the Azure portal, go to Microsoft Defender for Cloud and select *Regulatory compliance* from the left menu, as shown in the following screenshot:

Figure 4.11 Microsoft Defender for Cloud – Regulatory compliance

As shown in the preceding screenshot, the regulatory compliance dashboard helps customers track their compliance posture against industry standards such as `ISO 27001`, `SOC TSP`, `PCI DSS 3.2`, and Azure CIS. The dashboard lets customers view their compliance score and provides information about the number of assessments that pass and fail with each regulatory standard.

The regulatory compliance dashboard is a key feature of Microsoft Defender for Cloud, providing an overview of the customer's compliance posture across all regulatory standards. The dashboard provides customers with actionable insights, enabling them to focus on areas that require immediate attention. By identifying gaps in compliance, customers can improve their compliance posture and reduce the risk of non-compliance with industry regulations.

The regulatory compliance dashboard includes several features that help customers improve their compliance posture in alignment with the Microsoft cloud security benchmark, including the ability to resolve recommendations directly within the dashboard. Customers can click through each recommendation to discover details about the resources for which the recommendation should be implemented. The dashboard also provides a risk assessment summary, which highlights high-risk resources that require immediate attention, as shown in *Figure 4.12*:

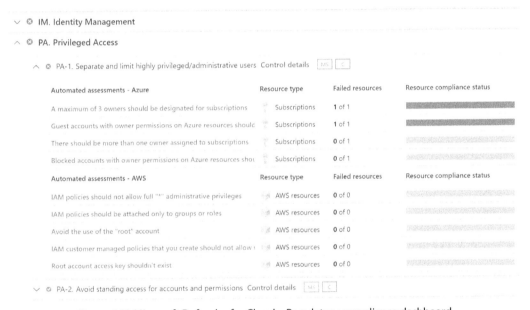

Figure 4.12 Microsoft Defender for Cloud – Regulatory compliance dashboard

The regulatory compliance dashboard is designed to help customers prepare for audits and assessments by providing evidence of their compliance status with industry standards. Customers can also generate reports that can be readily shared with stakeholders, providing visibility into the customer's compliance posture. The dashboard provides a comprehensive view of the customer's compliance status, enabling customers to demonstrate their commitment to compliance and improve their overall security posture.

As more businesses are moving their operations to the cloud, the need for effective cloud security solutions has become increasingly important. Microsoft Defender for Cloud is a cloud-native security solution that protects multi-cloud and hybrid environments.

In the next section, we will discuss capabilities such as endpoint detection and response, anti-malware, vulnerability assessment, and proactive threat hunting that Microsoft Defender for Cloud offers to enable comprehensive protection for workloads running on different cloud platforms. The solution uses machine learning and AI to detect and respond to security threats across multi-cloud environments, allowing security teams to identify the root cause of an attack and take remediation steps to prevent it from happening again.

Enabling visibility, detection, and response to threats using Microsoft Defender for Cloud

Microsoft Defender for Cloud is a cloud-native security solution that provides comprehensive protection for multi-cloud and hybrid environments. It offers several capabilities for securing workloads, including **endpoint detection and response** (EDR), anti-malware, vulnerability assessment, and proactive threat hunting. Defender for Cloud provides a unified view of security posture across multiple cloud platforms, enabling security teams to manage their security posture more effectively.

Microsoft Defender for Cloud protects workloads across cloud platforms such as Azure, AWS, and GCP. The solution offers native integration with these cloud platforms, seamlessly integrating with various cloud services. Defender for Cloud provides security insights, vulnerability assessments, and threat protection for workloads running on these cloud platforms.

Defender for Cloud uses machine learning and AI to detect and respond to security threats across multi-cloud environments. It offers proactive threat-hunting capabilities, which enable security teams to detect and respond to threats before they can cause any damage. With Defender for Cloud, security teams can identify the root cause of an attack, contain it, and take the necessary remediation steps to prevent it from happening again.

Defender for Cloud provides a single-pane-of-glass view of the security posture across multiple cloud platforms. This unified view makes it easier for security teams to monitor their security posture and take appropriate action when needed. It provides real-time insights into the security of workloads running on any of the cloud platforms, allowing security teams to quickly detect and respond to threats, as shown in *Figure 4.13*:

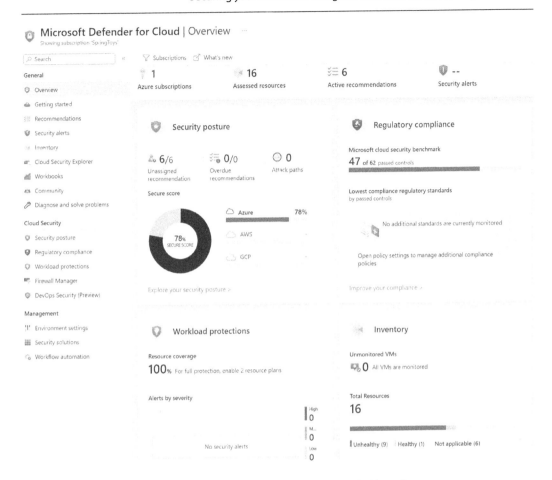

Figure 4.13 Microsoft Defender for Cloud dashboard

Defender for Cloud integrates with other Microsoft security solutions, such as Microsoft 365 Defender and Microsoft Sentinel, to provide comprehensive security across the entire IT environment.

Microsoft Defender for Cloud also provides security recommendations to help organizations improve their security posture in multi-cloud environments. These recommendations are based on Microsoft's best practices for securing cloud workloads and can be customized to meet the specific needs of each organization.

The recommendations cover various aspects of cloud security, including IAM, network security, data protection, and compliance, as shown in *Figure 4.14*:

Figure 4.14 Microsoft Defender for Cloud – Recommendations

As shown in the preceding figure, Defender for Cloud's security recommendations are presented in an easy-to-use dashboard that provides a summary of the organization's security posture and detailed information on each recommendation. The dashboard also provides an overview of the security risks associated with the organization's cloud workloads and recommendations for mitigating these risks. Organizations can prioritize the security recommendations based on their specific needs and capabilities and track progress in implementing these recommendations over time. The solution allows security teams to customize their security settings and policies according to their specific needs. Defender for Cloud also provides comprehensive protection for multi-cloud and hybrid environments. It provides a unified view of security posture across multiple cloud platforms and uses machine learning and AI to detect and respond to security threats across multi-cloud environments.

Check the following step-by-step guide for further information on Microsoft Defender:

`https://bit.ly/ms-defender-for-cloud-walkthrough`

Microsoft Defender also offers another set of features to help organizations detect and respond to identity-based attacks: Defender for Identity.

In the next section, we will review how Defender for Identity provides real-time visibility into the identity-related activities of users and their devices, enabling security teams to identify and respond to potential threats quickly.

Enhancing organizational security with Microsoft Defender for Identity

Microsoft Defender for Identity is a cloud-based security solution that helps organizations detect and respond to identity-based attacks in their on-premises and cloud environments. It provides a comprehensive view of the organization's identity-related risks and actionable insights to mitigate them. Defender for Identity uses machine learning algorithms to detect anomalies in user behavior, which can indicate potential security breaches.

Defender for Identity provides real-time visibility into the identity-related activities of users and their devices, enabling security teams to identify and respond to potential threats quickly. It integrates with Microsoft's Active Directory to provide advanced threat detection and remediation capabilities. Defender for Identity monitors user activity across the organization's entire IT environment, including on-premises, cloud, and hybrid environments.

Defender for Identity provides several key features to help organizations secure their identities. These features include advanced threat detection, identity analytics, and automated response capabilities. The solution also provides real-time alerts and reports, allowing security teams to respond quickly to potential threats.

One of the key benefits of Defender for Identity is its ability to detect and respond to advanced threats, such as Pass-the-Hash attacks, Golden Ticket attacks, and Kerberos compromises. It uses machine learning algorithms to identify anomalous user behavior, which can indicate an advanced attack. Defender for Identity also provides real-time monitoring of privileged accounts, which attackers often target.

You can try Defender for Identity by using the following URL:

```
https://bit.ly/try-defender-for-identity
```

Defender for Identity is part of the Microsoft Defender suite of security solutions, which includes Microsoft Defender for Endpoint and Microsoft Defender for Office 365. These solutions work together to provide a comprehensive security posture for organizations. Defender for Identity provides a centralized view of identity-related risks and can be used with the other Defender solutions to provide a complete picture of an organization's security posture.

Defender for Identity comprises three main components: the Microsoft 365 Defender portal, Defender for Identity sensor, and Defender for Identity cloud service.

The Microsoft 365 Defender portal creates and displays the Defender for Identity instance, enabling the monitoring, management, and investigation of threats. The Defender for Identity sensor can be installed on domain controllers and AD FS servers to monitor domain controller traffic, network traffic, and authentication events. And lastly, the Defender for Identity cloud service is deployed on Azure infrastructure and connected to Microsoft's intelligent security graph.

As cyber threats become increasingly sophisticated and frequent, organizations constantly search for reliable security solutions to protect their endpoints and devices. This is where Microsoft Defender for Endpoint comes in. It is a cloud-based security solution that provides comprehensive endpoint security protection against advanced threats, including file-based malware, fileless attacks, and ransomware. It offers a range of features, including advanced threat protection, post-breach detection and investigation capabilities, and endpoint monitoring across various operating systems.

In the next section, we will explore the key features and benefits of Microsoft Defender for Endpoint, as well as a real example of how it played a crucial role in protecting against the SolarWinds supply chain attack.

Protecting devices against advanced threats with Microsoft Defender for Endpoint

Microsoft Defender for Endpoint is a cloud-based security solution that helps organizations protect their devices and endpoints from cyber threats such as malware, viruses, and other advanced attacks. It provides a unified endpoint security platform that combines preventative protection, post-breach detection, automated investigation, and response capabilities. Defender for Endpoint is part of the Microsoft Defender suite of security solutions that also includes Microsoft Defender for Identity and Microsoft Defender for Office 365.

One of the critical features of Defender for Endpoint is its advanced threat protection capabilities. It uses artificial intelligence and machine learning algorithms to detect and block known and unknown threats in real time, including file-based malware, fileless attacks, and ransomware. It also includes behavioral analysis to detect and block suspicious activity and malicious behavior. Defender for Endpoint can also monitor and protect endpoints across all major operating systems, including Windows, macOS, Linux, and Android.

Another essential feature of Defender for Endpoint is its post-breach detection and investigation capabilities. In the event of a security breach, Defender for Endpoint provides detailed incident reports and forensic data to help security teams investigate and remediate the issue. It also includes automated investigation and remediation capabilities to help security teams quickly respond to security incidents and prevent further damage.

Defender for Endpoint could be used to protect against the SolarWinds supply chain attack. In late 2020, it was discovered that malicious actors had compromised the software supply chain of SolarWinds, a major IT management software vendor, and had inserted malware into its software updates. This malware, known as Sunburst, was distributed to numerous SolarWinds customers, including government agencies and major corporations.

Defender for Endpoint could detect and block the Sunburst malware on compromised devices, helping to limit the damage caused by the attack. It also provides detailed incident reports and forensic data to help security teams investigate an attack and remediate any issues. Additionally, Defender for Endpoint provides valuable threat intelligence to other security solutions in the Microsoft Defender suite, such as Microsoft Defender for Identity and Microsoft Defender for Office 365, helping to improve overall security across the organization.

Organizations can use Microsoft Defender for Endpoint to enable a comprehensive endpoint security solution that combines preventative protection, post-breach detection and investigation, and automated response capabilities.

The increasing use of cloud-based applications and services has increased the need for advanced security solutions to protect sensitive data and comply with regulatory requirements.

The next section will analyze how Microsoft Defender for Cloud Apps can provide advanced threat protection capabilities for cloud-based applications and services. It uses artificial intelligence and machine learning algorithms to detect and block various types of cyber threats in real time.

Defender for Cloud Apps also provides visibility and control over cloud applications and services, enabling organizations to monitor user activity, identify high-risk usage, and apply policies to prevent unauthorized access and data exfiltration. In this way, it helps organizations to secure sensitive data and meet regulatory requirements.

Securing sensitive data and meeting regulations with Microsoft Defender for Cloud Apps

Microsoft Defender for Cloud Apps, now part of Microsoft 365 Defender, is a cloud-native security solution designed to help organizations protect their cloud-based applications and services. It provides advanced threat protection capabilities to detect and block various types of cyber threats, including phishing attacks, account takeover, malware, and other advanced attacks. Defender for Cloud Apps is part of the Microsoft Defender suite of security solutions, including Microsoft Defender for Endpoint and Microsoft Defender for Identity.

One of the key features of Defender for Cloud Apps is its ability to provide visibility and control over cloud applications and services. It enables organizations to monitor user activity across cloud applications and services, identify high-risk usage, and apply policies to prevent unauthorized access and data exfiltration. It also integrates with other Microsoft security solutions to provide a unified view of security events and alerts. Defender for Cloud Apps uses artificial intelligence and machine learning algorithms to detect and block various types of cyber threats in real time. It can identify suspicious user behavior, such as failed logins, unauthorized access attempts, and unusual file access patterns. It can also detect malicious files and URLs and quarantine or block them before they can cause any damage.

Organizations can effectively secure their sensitive data and comply with regulatory requirements by using Microsoft Defender for Cloud Apps, a powerful security solution. This solution offers the following benefits:

- **Protect Sensitive Data**: Microsoft Defender for Cloud Apps can identify and classify sensitive data and apply appropriate security controls such as encryption, access controls, or data loss prevention policies.

- **Monitor for Threats**: Microsoft Defender for Cloud Apps can monitor for various cyber threats such as phishing attacks and malware. It can automatically remediate or alert security teams for further investigation when a threat is detected.

- **Meet Regulatory Compliance**: Microsoft Defender for Cloud Apps provides visibility into data access and usage, applies appropriate security controls, and generates audit logs for compliance reporting to meet regulatory requirements.

- **Integrate with Other Security Solutions**: Microsoft Defender for Cloud Apps can integrate with other security solutions, such as Microsoft Cloud App Security or Microsoft Information Protection, to provide a more comprehensive security posture.

- **Provide Actionable Insights**: Microsoft Defender for Cloud Apps can provide actionable insights into the security posture of your cloud environment by identifying vulnerabilities, providing recommendations for improving security controls, and tracking security incidents to help inform future security strategies.

A real example of how Defender for Cloud Apps can be used in practice is its role in protecting against phishing attacks on financial institutions. Consider a scenario in which the attack involved sending phishing emails to the institution's employees, aiming to steal their login credentials and gain access to the institution's cloud-based applications and services.

Defender for Cloud Apps can detect phishing emails and block them before they reach the targeted employees. It also alerts the security team to the attempted attack and provides detailed information on the type of attack, the number of users affected, and the potential impact. The security team would then be able to investigate the incident and take appropriate actions to prevent any further damage.

As organizations increasingly adopt hybrid cloud and edge environments, managing and securing infrastructure across disparate environments can be challenging. Azure Arc solves this challenge, offering a unified control plane for managing servers, Kubernetes clusters, and applications across on-premises, multi-cloud, and edge environments. With Azure Arc, organizations can take advantage of advanced security capabilities such as threat protection, compliance, and access control to secure their infrastructure and data.

The Microsoft Defender for Cloud Apps integration with Microsoft 365 Defender and the automatic redirection option is **Generally Available (GA)**: `https://bit.ly/defender-for-cloud-apps-updates`.

The following section will explore using Azure Arc to provide a comprehensive security solution for hybrid cloud and edge environments.

Secure infrastructure everywhere: Deploying hybrid security solutions from the cloud to the edge

Azure Arc is a hybrid cloud management solution that provides a unified control plane for managing servers across data centers and multi-cloud environments, Kubernetes clusters, and applications across on-premises, multi-cloud, and edge environments. Azure Arc also offers advanced security capabilities to help organizations secure their infrastructure and data across these environments.

One of the key security features of Azure Arc is its ability to provide a unified view of security across all connected servers and Kubernetes clusters. This enables organizations to monitor security events and vulnerabilities across their entire infrastructure and take appropriate actions to mitigate risks.

Azure Arc also integrates with Microsoft Defender for Cloud, which provides advanced threat protection capabilities for servers and Kubernetes clusters. Another key security feature of Azure Arc is its ability to provide granular access controls for servers and Kubernetes clusters. Organizations can define role-based access policies for different user groups and enforce multi-factor authentication to prevent unauthorized access. Azure Arc also supports integration with Azure AD for identity and access management.

As organizations adopt cloud and edge computing technologies, deploying hybrid security solutions has become increasingly important. Here are some tips for deploying a hybrid security solution that can help secure your infrastructure from the cloud to the edge:

- Define your security requirements: Identify assets, assess risks, and define security policies before deploying a hybrid security solution.

- Implement a centralized security management system: Implement a centralized security management system to monitor and manage security policies across your entire infrastructure.

- Use a multilayered security approach: Employ a multilayered security approach that includes firewalls, intrusion detection and prevention systems, antivirus software, and other security technologies.

- Deploy security controls at the edge: Deploy security controls, such as firewalls, encryption, and other security technologies, at the edge to protect edge computing devices and sensors, which are often the first point of contact for attacks.

- Use cloud-based security services: Extend security controls beyond your on-premises infrastructure to the cloud by using cloud-based firewalls, intrusion detection and prevention systems, and other security services.

- Implement security analytics: Use security analytics, such as machine learning algorithms or security information and event management (SIEM) systems, to detect and respond to security threats in real time.

Deploying a hybrid security solution requires a multilayered approach that uses centralized security management, edge security controls, cloud-based security services, and security analytics. By adopting these strategies, you can help secure your infrastructure from the cloud to the edge.

Azure Arc provides a comprehensive security solution for managing and securing servers and Kubernetes clusters across hybrid cloud and edge environments. Its advanced threat protection, compliance, and access control features enable organizations to maintain a secure and compliant infrastructure while taking advantage of the benefits of the hybrid cloud.

Security becomes a top priority as more organizations adopt cloud-based solutions such as Microsoft Azure Kubernetes Service (AKS) to deploy, scale, and manage containerized applications.

AKS has several built-in features to enhance security for the cluster and applications running on it, including network security, authentication, and access control. AKS can be integrated with Microsoft Defender for Containers, a comprehensive security solution that provides vulnerability management, and runtime protection to enhance security for containerized applications further.

In the next section, we will discuss how organizations can better protect their AKS clusters from threats and vulnerabilities and ensure a more secure container environment for their applications.

Securing your Kubernetes clusters in Azure: protecting against threats and vulnerabilities

AKS is a managed Kubernetes service that's used to deploy, scale, and manage containerized applications. Security is a crucial concern for any cloud-based service, and AKS has several features that help to enhance security for the cluster and applications running on it.

The first line of defense is network security. AKS supports virtual networks, **network security groups** (**NSGs**), and Azure Firewall to create a secure network perimeter. AKS also uses Azure AD to authenticate users and control resource access.

To secure the container images that AKS uses, **Azure Container Registry** (**ACR**) is integrated with AKS. ACR provides secure storage and management of container images and scanning and vulnerability assessment tools to ensure that images are free of vulnerabilities and malware.

AKS also includes several features for securing the Kubernetes control plane, including RBAC, Azure Private Link, and Azure Policy. RBAC enables administrators to control access to Kubernetes resources, while Azure Private Link allows secure access to the control plane over a private network. Azure Policy provides a centralized way to enforce governance and compliance across the cluster.

AKS provides several options for securing applications running on the cluster, including network security policies and pod security policies, and it can be integrated with Defender for Containers.

Microsoft Defender for Containers is designed to provide comprehensive protection for containerized applications running in AKS and other container environments. It includes several features to enhance container security, including vulnerability management and runtime protection.

Vulnerability management is a crucial component of Defender for Containers, providing continuous assessment and scanning of container images for known vulnerabilities and malware. The solution also includes an image scanning pipeline that integrates with ACR to scan images during the build process.

Runtime protection is another important feature, providing real-time monitoring and threat detection for containers running in AKS and other environments. This includes file integrity monitoring, network security policies, and behavioral analysis to detect anomalous behavior.

Defender for Containers can be enabled using the Azure portal. In the Defender for Cloud service, the Defender for Containers plan can be turned on, as shown in *Figure 4.15*:

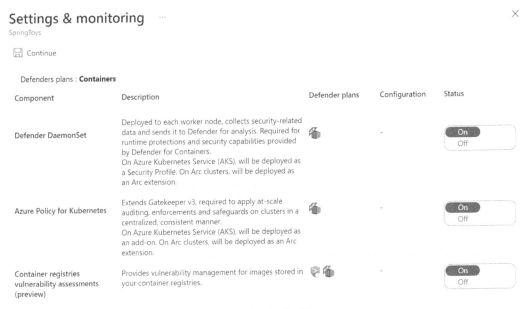

Figure 4.15 Defender for Containers

Defender for Containers provides a unified view of security across the container environment. This allows administrators to view security alerts and recommendations for improving security across the entire environment, including AKS clusters and other container environments.

Microsoft Defender for Containers offers cluster-level and node-level threat protection. It provides security alerts by monitoring the control plane and the containerized workload. Control plane alerts can be identified by a prefix of K8S_ in the alert type, while runtime workload alerts have a prefix of K8S.NODE_.

You can check the complete list of alerts at https://bit.ly/az-alerts-aks.

In conclusion, AKS offers a wide range of security features to ensure the safety and protection of containerized applications deployed on the cloud. AKS provides network, container image, and control plane security through integration with ACR and Microsoft Defender for Containers. Defender for Containers offers a unified view of security across the container environment with continuous assessment and scanning for vulnerabilities and malware, real-time monitoring and threat detection, and cluster-level and node-level threat protection. Administrators can view security alerts and recommendations for improving security across the entire environment, making it a comprehensive security solution for AKS clusters and other container environments.

Summary

This chapter covered the Azure security benefits for organizations, including identity and access management and best practices for securing workloads on Azure. Microsoft Sentinel was also discussed as a tool for intelligent security analytics and threat intelligence across the enterprise.

The Microsoft cloud security benchmark was introduced as a resource for security recommendations on Azure workloads. Microsoft Defender for Cloud was introduced as a solution for threat visibility, detection, and response across multiple cloud platforms. Additionally, we discussed Microsoft Defender for Identity and Microsoft Defender for Endpoint, which are tools for identifying suspicious activity and preventing advanced targeted attacks.

Finally, Microsoft Defender for Cloud Apps was presented as a way to enable visibility and control over cloud usage for protecting sensitive data and regulatory compliance. The importance of data protection and the role of IAM solutions in ensuring the security and privacy of organizational data was also discussed.

We covered **Infrastructure as Code (IaC)**, which has become an increasingly popular approach to deploying and managing infrastructure in the cloud. In the next chapter, we will discuss the reasons for using IaC in Azure, the benefits of IaC, and the different IaC frameworks that are available. We will also look at some best practices for using IaC in Azure, including using Azure DevOps and GitHub. Additionally, we will explore Azure governance, its benefits, and the various Azure governance tools, such as Azure Blueprints and Azure Policy.

5

Automation and Governance in Azure

Azure provides a wide range of services and tools that enable organizations to deploy, run, and manage their applications and services in the cloud. Naturally, we can go to the Azure portal and manually create any Azure resources via the portal user interface. However, when you need to provision and manage resources for a complex infrastructure that spans multiple environments and regions, performing these tasks manually can be cumbersome.

This is where automation and governance come in. With automation, we can use **Infrastructure as Code (IaC)** to develop reusable recipes that define our infrastructure and automate its deployment across multiple environments in a consistent manner. With IaC, we can save a lot of time in carrying out repetitive deployments. With governance, we can ensure that our Azure environments meet compliance, security, and operational requirements.

We will begin by looking at IaC and exploring why it is essential for automating the provisioning of Azure resources and infrastructure.

In this chapter, we will cover the following topics:

- Using IaC for resource management
- Microsoft-native IaC frameworks
- Automation with Azure DevOps and GitHub
- Azure governance

Automate provisioning of Azure resources using IaC

IaC is an essential tool for managing infrastructure in a cloud computing environment such as Azure. IaC is a methodology for managing and provisioning infrastructure through code. It is a critical component of modern infrastructure management. It enables development teams to automate the process of creating, configuring, and managing infrastructure, making it easier to deploy and manage applications and services.

Streamline infrastructure management with IaC

IaC helps you manage infrastructure at scale by enabling you to define infrastructure as templates that can be deployed automatically. With IaC, you can manage complex infrastructure more easily and respond to changes on demand.

Here are some additional reasons why you need IaC:

- **Consistency**: IaC enables development teams to create and manage infrastructure in a consistent and repeatable way. This reduces the risk of errors and inconsistencies and improves the overall quality of infrastructure.

  Since the infrastructure is defined as code, the code can be checked into version control systems, tested, and deployed automatically across multiple environments. This ensures that your infrastructure is consistent and reproducible across environments, which reduces the risk of errors and misconfigurations.

- **Efficiency**: IaC can help you reduce the time and effort required to manage infrastructure by automating tasks such as provisioning, configuration, and deployment. This allows you to focus on more strategic work and reduces the risk of human error.

- **Speed**: IaC enables teams to automate the process of creating and configuring infrastructure in a quick and repeatable manner. This can reduce the time it takes to provision infrastructure and help you respond to changes in demand or business requirements faster. This automation also speeds up the development process and enables development teams to deliver new features and fixes to customers more quickly.

- **Scalability**: IaC enables teams to quickly and easily scale infrastructure up or down as needed, based on changing demand. You can define your IaC and then use automation to quickly deploy and manage resources on Azure. This helps organizations to stay agile and responsive to changing customer needs.

- **Collaboration**: IaC promotes collaboration between developers, testers, and operations teams. This collaboration helps to break down silos and enables teams to work more efficiently and effectively.

  IaC makes it easier for teams to collaborate on infrastructure management, as code can be shared and reviewed in version control systems. This helps to improve communication and reduce the risk of misunderstandings.

  IaC enables teams to work collaboratively by sharing code and infrastructure definitions. This can improve communication and reduce the risk of miscommunication or errors.

- **Security**: IaC can improve security by enabling consistent security policies across environments and ensuring that security updates are applied consistently and in a timely manner.

- **Cost savings**: IaC can helMp you reduce costs by enabling you to provision and deprovision infrastructure quickly and automatically, ensuring that you only pay for what you really need.

In the next section, we will talk about the principles of IaC that development teams should follow.

Principles of IaC

IaC is a key DevOps practice and a component of continuous delivery. With IaC, DevOps teams can work together with a unified set of practices and tools to deliver applications and their supporting infrastructure rapidly and reliably at scale.

To get the most out of IaC, development teams should follow these principles:

- **Declarative definition**: IaC uses a declarative definition of infrastructure resources, which describes the desired state of the infrastructure rather than the steps needed to create it. This approach allows easier maintenance and repeatability, as changes to the infrastructure can be made by modifying the code rather than making manual changes.

- **Version control**: IaC treats infrastructure resources as code and manages them using version control systems, such as Git. This allows teams to track changes, collaborate with others, and undo changes if necessary.

- **Idempotent**: IaC code should be idempotent, meaning that it can be run multiple times without changing the state of the infrastructure. This enables teams to easily make changes and roll back if necessary.

- **Testing**: IaC code should be thoroughly tested to ensure that it is working as intended and to catch and fix errors before they reach production environments. This includes testing for performance, security, and functionality.

- **Automation**: IaC emphasizes automation, using tools and scripts to automatically create and manage infrastructure resources. This improves efficiency and reduces errors, as manual intervention is minimized.

- **Reusability**: IaC promotes reusability by allowing you to define infrastructure resources as modular components that can be used across different projects and environments. This reduces duplication and simplifies maintenance.

- **Consistency**: IaC ensures consistency across infrastructure resources by enforcing a standardized approach to their definition and deployment. This improves reliability and reduces the likelihood of errors caused by differences in configuration.

In the next section, we will talk about both native Microsoft and third-party IaC frameworks.

Microsoft-native IaC frameworks

There are many IaC frameworks that can be used on Azure. In this chapter, we will focus mainly on out-of-the-box Microsoft IaC solutions, namely **Azure Resource Manager (ARM)** templates and Bicep.

Azure Resource Manager (ARM) templates

ARM templates are a declarative way to define and deploy Azure resources. ARM templates use JSON syntax to define resources and their properties, making it easy to manage and deploy infrastructure changes.

We will learn more about ARM templates in the following sections.

Accelerate deployment with ARM templates

The real benefit of using the ARM template system is that it allows you to have declarative syntax. That means you can deploy a virtual machine and create the networking infrastructure that goes around it. Templates end up providing a process that can be run repeatedly in a very consistent manner. They manage the desired state of the infrastructure, meaning a template becomes the source of truth for those infrastructure resources. If you make changes to your infrastructure, you should do that through ARM templates.

We will highlight some of the other key benefits of using ARM templates to deploy resources in Azure:

- **Consistency**: By defining ARM templates, you can ensure that your resources are deployed consistently across all environments. This can help to reduce errors and increase reliability.

- **Automation**: ARM templates allow you to automate your deployment process, reducing the time and effort required to deploy your resources. You can also use scripts to automate the deployment of your templates.

- **Reusability**: By defining variables and templates, you can create reusable templates that can be used to deploy similar resources in different environments. This can help you to save time and reduce the risk of errors.

- **Scalability**: ARM templates allow you to easily scale your resources up or down, depending on your needs. This can help you to optimize your costs and ensure that you have the resources you need when you need them.

- **Version control**: ARM templates can be versioned and stored in source control, allowing you to easily track changes to your infrastructure over time. This can help you to troubleshoot issues and roll back changes if necessary.

- **Security**: ARM templates allow you to define security and access policies for your resources during deployment, ensuring that your resources are secured from the outset.

- **Cost optimization**: ARM templates can help you to optimize your costs by allowing you to deploy only the resources that you need and providing visibility into your resource usage.

ARM templates provide a powerful way to define and deploy resources in Azure. By using ARM templates, you can automate your deployment process, ensure consistency across environments, simplify the management of your infrastructure, and optimize your costs.

Deep dive into ARM templates

ARM is the primary management tool for deploying and managing resources on Azure.

ARM templates are a declarative way to define your IaC. ARM templates can be used to deploy a wide variety of resources in Azure, including virtual machines, storage accounts, and virtual networks. ARM templates help teams take a more agile approach to deploying infrastructure in the cloud; it is no longer necessary to manually click within the Azure portal to create your infrastructure.

ARM templates allow you to define the infrastructure and configuration for your application in a JSON file, which can then be deployed consistently across multiple environments. This enables you to manage your resources in a more consistent and repeatable way, improving efficiency and reducing the risk of misconfiguration.

Here is an example of an ARM template in JSON format for provisioning a storage account:

```
{
  "$schema": "https://schema.management.azure.com/schemas/2019-04-01/
deploymentTemplate.json#",
  "contentVersion": "1.0.0.0",
  "parameters": {
    "location": {
      "type": "string",
      "defaultValue": "[resourceGroup().location]"
    },
    "storageAccountName": {
      "type": "string",
      "defaultValue": "[format(storageAcct{0}',
uniqueString(resourceGroup().id))]"
    }
  },
  "resources": [
    {
      "type": "Microsoft.Storage/storageAccounts",
      "apiVersion": "2021-06-01",
      "name": "[parameters('storageAccountName')]",
      "location": "[parameters('location')]",
      "sku": {
        "name": "Standard_LRS"
      },
      "kind": "StorageV2",
```

```
    "properties": {
      "accessTier": "Hot"
    }
  }
 ]

}
```

By using ARM templates, you can automate your deployment process using Azure DevOps or GitHub, as we will explore in later sections. You can use ARM templates in **continuous integration** and **continuous deployment (CI/CD)** pipelines and code deployment to build a suite of applications within the organization. This ensures that your infrastructure is consistent across all environments.

ARM templates tend to be quite verbose due to their JSON syntax. As a best practice, you should always look for opportunities to break large ARM template files into smaller files. From a maintainability standpoint, this practice allows smaller ARM templates to be linked as reusable components in other ARM templates.

To learn more about ARM templates, visit:

https://learn.microsoft.com/azure/azure-resource-manager/templates/overview

Bicep

Despite their greatness, ARM templates do have some challenges and limitations, such as verbosity, complex syntax, and difficulty in authoring and maintaining them.

Bicep was created to address the challenges and limitations of ARM templates. Bicep is a **Domain-Specific Language (DSL)** and an open-source project from Microsoft that provides a more concise and user-friendly way to define ARM templates.

Boost productivity and efficiency with Bicep

Bicep is designed to be easier to read, write, and maintain than ARM templates. It provides full backward compatibility with ARM templates. It is essentially a higher-level abstraction of ARM templates that allows you to write IaC in a more declarative and readable way.

Bicep provides all the benefits that we stated earlier for ARM templates, plus the following:

- **Simplicity**: Bicep has a cleaner syntax, which reduces the amount of code required to define Azure resources. It also provides a more structured and modular way to author templates, which makes them easier to read, write, and maintain.

- **Reusability**: Bicep allows you to define reusable modules that can be used across multiple templates. This simplifies the process of creating and maintaining templates and can help to reduce errors and improve consistency.

- **Type safety**: Bicep is a strongly typed language that provides type safety and compile-time checks, which helps to catch errors earlier in the development process.

- **Modularity**: You can break your Bicep code into manageable parts by using modules. Modules deploy a set of related resources. They enable you to reuse code and simplify development. Add a module to a Bicep file anytime you need to deploy those resources.

- **Azure integration**: Bicep is designed specifically for Azure and provides a set of tools and features that make it easy to integrate with Azure services and resources.

- **Open source**: Bicep is an open-source project that is actively developed and maintained by Microsoft. This ensures that it will continue to evolve and improve over time.

- **Improved readability**: Bicep uses a simplified syntax that is easier to read and understand than JSON-based ARM templates. The code is structured in a way that makes it easier to identify resources, properties, and dependencies, reducing the risk of errors.

- **Increased productivity**: With Bicep, developers can write less code to accomplish the same tasks as ARM templates, which reduces the time and effort required to deploy resources. Bicep also provides features such as parameter sets and modules that simplify code reuse and promote consistency.

- **Better collaboration**: Bicep provides a simplified and unified syntax that can be easily shared and understood by different members of a team, including developers, infrastructure engineers, and security professionals. This promotes better collaboration and communication across teams, reducing the risk of errors and improving the speed of deployment.

- **Improved maintainability**: With Bicep, developers can more easily maintain and update their code as changes are made to the infrastructure. Bicep supports modular design patterns that promote code reuse, and it can be easily versioned and managed using source control tools such as Git.

- **Repeatable results**: Repeatedly deploy your infrastructure throughout the development lifecycle and have confidence that your resources are deployed in a consistent manner. Bicep files are idempotent, which means you can deploy the same file many times and get the same resource types in the same state. You can develop one file that represents the desired state, rather than developing lots of separate files to represent updates.

- **No state or state files to manage**: All states are stored in Azure. Users can collaborate and have confidence that their updates are handled as expected.

- **Greater control and consistency**: With Bicep, developers can define resource dependencies and deployment order, which can help prevent errors and ensure that resources are deployed in the correct sequence. Bicep also supports validation and linting tools that can help identify potential errors or issues before deployment.

In summary, Bicep is a user-friendly and concise language that simplifies the authoring and maintenance of ARM templates. It provides a variety of benefits over ARM templates, including simplicity, reusability, type safety, Azure integration, and open source development.

Deep dive into Bicep

Here is the Bicep version of the same ARM template that we illustrated earlier for provisioning a storage account:

```
param location string = resourceGroup().location
param storageAccountName string =
storageAcct${uniqueString(resourceGroup().id)}'

resource storageAccount 'Microsoft.Storage/storageAccounts@2021-06-01'
= {
  name: storageAccountName
  location: location
  sku: {
    name: 'Standard_LRS'
  }
  kind: 'StorageV2'
  properties: {
    accessTier: 'Hot'
  }

}
```

As you can see, Bicep is a syntax-friendly language that simplifies the authoring of ARM templates. Best of all, Bicep has the capability to transpile into native ARM template code.

To learn more about Bicep, visit:

```
https://learn.microsoft.com/azure/azure-resource-manager/bicep/
overview
```

Popular third-party IaC frameworks

Before we move on, it is worth mentioning some of the popular third-party IaC frameworks that you can also use to provision Azure resources:

- **Terraform** is an open-source IaC tool that supports Azure and other cloud providers. It uses a declarative language called **HashiCorp Configuration Language** (HCL) to define infrastructure and has a large community of contributors.

  ```
  https://www.terraform.io/
  ```

- **Ansible** is an open-source automation tool that can be used for IaC on Azure. It uses a declarative language called YAML to define infrastructure and is known for its simplicity and ease of use.

  ```
  https://www.ansible.com/
  ```

- **Chef** is an open-source configuration management tool that can be used for IaC on Azure. It uses a declarative language called **Chef Infra Language** (**CIL**) to define infrastructure and has a large community of contributors.

  `https://www.chef.io/`

- **Puppet** is an open-source configuration management tool that can be used for IaC on Azure. It uses a declarative language called Puppet DSL to define infrastructure and is known for its scalability and flexibility.

  `https://www.puppet.com/`

- **Pulumi** is an open-source and cloud-agnostic IaC framework that allows you to define infrastructure using familiar programming languages such as Python, JavaScript, TypeScript, and Go. It offers native support for Azure and other cloud providers, enabling you to provision and manage resources using your preferred programming language.

  `https://www.pulumi.com/`

- **AWS CloudFormation**, primarily associated with **Amazon Web Services** (**AWS**), can also be used for Azure resource provisioning using ARM templates. CloudFormation provides a JSON- or YAML-based template format for defining infrastructure and supports advanced features such as nested stacks, resource dependencies, and stack updates.

  `https://aws.amazon.com/cloudformation/`

All of these IaC frameworks provide different features and capabilities, so it is important to choose the one that best fits your organization's needs. Each of these frameworks has its own strengths and weaknesses, and you should consider factors such as your team's experience, the complexity of your infrastructure, and your organization's requirements when choosing an IaC framework on Azure.

Automate ARM templates and Bicep with Azure DevOps and GitHub

Azure DevOps and GitHub are both popular platforms for managing software development projects and collaborating on code.

Azure DevOps is a comprehensive set of tools and services for building, testing, and deploying applications and infrastructure on Azure. It provides a powerful platform for DevOps teams to manage their entire application lifecycle, from planning and coding to testing, deployment, and monitoring. Azure DevOps includes several components, such as Azure Repos, Azure Pipelines, Azure Boards, Azure Test Plans, and Azure Artifacts, which can be used independently or together to automate various aspects of the DevOps process.

GitHub is a web-based hosting service for version control using Git. Similar to Azure DevOps, GitHub provides a platform for collaborative development and allows developers to host and review code, manage projects, and build software.

Azure DevOps and GitHub provide similar benefits, including the following:

- **Version control**: Azure DevOps and GitHub provide version control for your ARM templates and Bicep files, allowing you to track changes, collaborate with others, and revert changes if necessary. This helps to ensure that your infrastructure code is consistent and reliable.

- **Continuous integration and deployment**: Azure DevOps and GitHub support CI/CD, which allows you to automate the testing and deployment of your ARM templates and Bicep files. This helps to ensure that changes are tested and deployed quickly and reliably.

- **Collaboration**: Azure DevOps and GitHub provide collaboration features, such as pull requests and code reviews, which allow you to work together with your team to improve the quality of your ARM templates and Bicep files.

- **Security**: Azure DevOps and GitHub provide security features, such as access controls and secret management, which help to ensure that your infrastructure code is secure, protected, and only accessible to authorized team members.

- **Integration with other tools**: Azure DevOps and GitHub integrate with a wide range of other tools, such as build systems, testing frameworks, and deployment tools, which allows you to customize your CI/CD pipeline to meet your specific needs.

Best practices for using Azure DevOps and GitHub for IaC on Azure

Overall, using Azure DevOps or GitHub with ARM templates and Bicep files can help to improve the quality, reliability, and efficiency of your infrastructure code. These platforms provide version control, CI/CD, collaboration, security, and integration features that are essential for managing infrastructure resources at scale.

Here are some best practices for using Azure DevOps and GitHub for IaC on Azure:

- **Use version control**: Manage changes to your IaC code using version control. This allows developers to track changes, collaborate with others, and revert to previous versions if necessary.

- **Use branching**: Manage different stages of your IaC code, such as development, testing, and production, by using branching. This allows you to test changes before deploying them to production, reducing the risk of errors and downtime.

- **Use pull requests**: With pull requests, review and approve changes to your IaC code. This allows you to ensure that changes are reviewed and approved by team members before they are merged into the main branch.

- **Continuous integration and continuous deployment**: Use Azure Pipelines or GitHub Actions to automate the deployment of your IaC code. These tools allow developers to automate the deployment of infrastructure code, reducing the time it takes to deploy infrastructure.

- **Test your IaC code in a non-production environment**: Before promoting to the production environment, always test your IaC code in a non-production environment to validate your IaC code and ensure that it works as expected. This can help you to reduce errors and ensure that your Azure environment is stable and secure before going to production.

By following these best practices, you can use Azure DevOps and GitHub for IaC on Azure more effectively to automate your resource and infrastructure deployment.

With our discussion on automation wrapped up, we'll now turn our focus to governance on Azure.

Improve governance with Azure

As we learned in the previous sections, it is essential to automate the provisioning of our infrastructure to improve consistency and reliability across Azure environments. In this section, we will learn the importance of governance on Azure and how it ensures that our Azure environment meets compliance, security, and operational requirements.

Here are some reasons why governance on Azure is important:

- **Compliance**: Compliance with regulatory requirements is critical for organizations in industries such as healthcare, finance, and government. Implementing governance policies and controls can help ensure that your Azure environment meets regulatory requirements.

- **Security**: For organizations moving to the cloud, security is a top concern. Implementing governance policies and controls can help you to protect your Azure environment from security threats and reduce the risk of data breaches and cyber-attacks.

- **Cost management**: Azure can be complex and difficult to manage, leading to cost overruns and budget issues. Implementing governance policies and controls can help you to optimize your Azure usage, reduce costs, and manage your budget effectively.

- **Operational efficiency**: Implementing governance policies and controls can help you to manage your Azure environment more efficiently, reducing the time and effort required for manual management tasks.

- **Risk management**: Implementing governance policies and controls can help you to manage risk by ensuring that your Azure environment is secure, compliant, and well managed.

By implementing governance on Azure, you can help ensure that your Azure environment is secure, compliant, and well managed, reducing the risk of security threats and data breaches, optimizing costs, and improving operational efficiency.

In the next section, we will look at ways of implementing governance on Azure.

Implement governance on Azure

Governance on Azure involves implementing policies, processes, and controls to ensure that your Azure environment meets compliance, security, and operational requirements.

Here are some steps to consider when implementing governance on Azure.

Implement Azure Policy

Azure Policy is a service that enables you to create, assign, and manage policies to enforce governance across your organization. You can use Azure Policy to define rules for resource types, locations, and tags, and enforce compliance with regulatory requirements, security standards, and other organizational policies.

Azure Policy provides a centralized way to manage policies and monitor compliance across your organization. You can create policies using Azure Policy's built-in policy definitions, customize policy definitions to meet your specific requirements, and create initiatives that group related policies. You can also create custom policies that are specific to your organization's needs. Policies can be used to enforce security controls, ensure compliance with regulatory requirements, or enforce organizational standards.

Azure Policy works by evaluating resources against the defined policies and reporting on any non-compliance. It can also take automated actions, such as blocking or remediation, to enforce compliance.

To learn more about Azure Policy, visit:

```
https://learn.microsoft.com/azure/governance/policy/overview
```

Define Azure Blueprints

Azure Blueprints is a service that allows you to define a repeatable set of Azure resources that can be deployed quickly and consistently across multiple environments. It enables you to define a set of Azure resources, including policies and configurations, that can be managed as a single unit.

Azure Blueprints provides a way to automate the creation, management, and governance of resources, and it helps ensure compliance with organizational standards and policies. It allows you to define a set of pre-built templates, called blueprints, which can be used to create environments that meet your specific requirements.

With Azure Blueprints, you can define a set of policies that govern the use of Azure resources and ensure compliance with regulatory and security requirements. You can also use Azure Blueprints to deploy resources across multiple Azure subscriptions and tenants, simplifying the management of complex environments.

Azure Blueprints provides a way to automate the deployment and management of resources, improving consistency and reducing the time and effort required to deploy and manage resources. It allows organizations to define standard patterns and templates that can be used across multiple teams and projects, helping to improve efficiency and reduce errors.

To learn more about Azure Blueprints, visit:

`https://learn.microsoft.com/azure/governance/blueprints/overview`

Use role-based access control (RBAC)

Use RBAC to manage access to Azure resources. RBAC allows you to assign permissions to users and groups based on their roles and responsibilities, helping you to control access and manage risk.

To learn more about RBAC, visit:

`https://learn.microsoft.com/azure/role-based-access-control/overview`

Monitor and audit your Azure environment

Use Azure Monitor to monitor and audit your Azure environment. Azure Monitor provides metrics, logs, and alerts that can help you detect and respond to security threats, compliance issues, and operational problems.

To learn more about Azure Monitor, visit:

`https://learn.microsoft.com/azure/azure-monitor/overview`

Use Azure Advisor

Use Azure Advisor to optimize your Azure environment for performance, reliability, and cost. Azure Advisor provides recommendations for optimizing resource configuration, improving security, and reducing costs.

`https://learn.microsoft.com/azure/advisor/advisor-overview`

Analyze your cloud inventory with Azure Resource Graph

Azure Resource Graph is a powerful management tool to query, explore, and analyze your cloud resources at scale. It allows you to quickly and efficiently query across Azure subscriptions. You can analyze your cloud inventory using complex queries launched programmatically or from the Azure portal and assess the impact of applying policies in large cloud environments.

`https://azure.microsoft.com/get-started/azure-portal/resource-graph/`

Manage your cloud spending

The Microsoft Cost Management tool allows you to monitor, allocate, and optimize cloud costs with transparency, accuracy, and efficiency. You can optimize your cloud investments, reduce costs, and increase the efficiency of your cloud investments. Furthermore, you can implement financial governance in your organization by focusing on visibility, accountability, and optimization.

```
https://azure.microsoft.com/products/cost-management/
```

By following these steps, you can implement governance on Azure to ensure compliance, security, and operational efficiency. As a best practice, we will talk about the five disciplines of cloud governance in the next section.

Five disciplines of cloud governance

Cloud governance is a set of policies, procedures, and best practices that organizations use to manage their cloud environments effectively. The five disciplines of cloud governance are a set of common governance disciplines that help form policies and align toolchains. This framework has been developed by various organizations and experts in the field of cloud computing and governance. In the Azure ecosystem, the five disciplines of cloud governance (see *Figure 5.1*) are defined as follows:

Govern   **Define Corporate Policy**

Business Risks   **Policy & Compliance**   **Process**

Document evolving business   Convert risk decisions   Establish processes to
risks and the business'   into policy statements   monitor violations and
tolerance for risk, based   to establish cloud   adherence to corporate
on data classification and   adoption boundaries   policies
application criticality

Five Disciplines of Cloud Governance

Cost   **Security**   **Resource**   **Identity**   **Deployment**
Management   **Baseline**   **Consistency**   **Baseline**   **Acceleration**

Evaluate and monitor Ensure compliance   Ensure consistency   Ensure the baseline Accelerate
costs, limit IT spend, with IT security   in resource   for identity and   deployment through
scale to meet need,   requirements by   configuration.   access are enforced centralization,
create cost   applying a security Enforce practices   by consistently   consistency, and
accountability   baseline to all   for on-boarding,   applying role   standardization
                      adoption efforts   recovery, and   definitions and   across deployment
                                          discoverability   assignments   templates

Figure 5.1: Five disciplines of cloud governance

- **Cost management**: Controlling spending is top of mind for all organizations. Cost management focuses on evaluating and monitoring costs, limiting IT spending, scaling to meet needs, and creating cost accountability.

  ```
  https://learn.microsoft.com/azure/cloud-adoption-framework/
  govern/cost-management/
  ```

- **Security baseline**: Ensure compliance with IT security requirements by applying a security baseline to all adoption efforts, such as network, data, and asset configurations.

  ```
  https://learn.microsoft.com/azure/cloud-adoption-framework/
  govern/security-baseline/
  ```

- **Resource consistency**: Using governance tooling, resources can be configured consistently to mitigate risks associated with onboarding, recovery, drift, and discoverability.

- ```
  https://learn.microsoft.com/azure/cloud-adoption-framework/
  govern/resource-consistency/
  ```

- **Identity baseline**: The identity baseline focuses on ensuring the baseline for identity and access is enforced by consistently applying role definitions and assignments.

- ```
  https://learn.microsoft.com/azure/cloud-adoption-framework/
  govern/identity-baseline/
  ```

- **Deployment acceleration**: Accelerate deployment through centralization, consistency, and standardization across deployment templates.

  ```
  https://learn.microsoft.com/azure/cloud-adoption-framework/
  govern/deployment-acceleration/
  ```

The five disciplines of cloud governance help guide decisions on the proper level of automation and the enforcement of an organizational policy in Azure.

With this, we wrap up our exploration of automation and governance in Azure.

Summary

In this chapter, we learned about the importance of automation and governance. We learned about the principles of IaC and took a deep dive into the two native Microsoft IaC frameworks: ARM templates and Bicep. By following the principles of IaC and using the right tools, development teams can take advantage of the many benefits of IaC, including consistency, speed, scalability, and collaboration. After that, we saw how Azure DevOps and GitHub can help efficiently automate the deployment of ARM templates and Bicep files.

We also learned that governance is a critical aspect of managing resources on Azure. It enables organizations to ensure compliance with regulatory requirements, security standards, and other organizational policies. Azure provides a range of services and tools to enable effective governance on the platform. We then talked about the five disciplines of cloud governance, which are best practices.

Automation and governance can help organizations streamline their operations and mitigate risks. At the same time, they enable compliance with governance policies and organizational standards.

The next chapter covers how you can maximize efficiency and cost savings in Azure.

Maximizing Efficiency and Cost Savings in Azure

In the world of cloud computing, cost optimization is becoming increasingly important. With the growing demand for cloud-based services, organizations are looking for ways to manage their cloud costs and maximize the value of their investments.

When it comes to designing a cloud-based architecture that is both efficient and cost-effective, the Microsoft Azure Well-Architected Framework provides a comprehensive set of guidelines and best practices.

Good architecture is not just a nice-to-have feature in the world of cloud computing; it is a fundamental aspect that can drive significant cost savings. With the increasing demand for cloud-based services, organizations cannot afford to overlook the importance of optimizing costs and maximizing their investments. That's why it is crucial to implement the cost optimization pillar of the Microsoft Azure Well-Architected Framework.

This chapter will cover the following topics, with a focus on optimizing costs in the cloud:

- Utilizing the cost optimization pillar of the Microsoft Azure Well-Architected Framework to design an efficient cloud-based architecture
- Incorporating Azure Advisor best practice recommendations for cost savings
- Implementing cost management best practices
- Effective budgeting for Azure services

Cost optimization with the Microsoft Azure Well-Architected Framework

Within the Microsoft Azure Well-Architected Framework, the cost optimization pillar identifies ways to reduce expenses without sacrificing performance or functionality. With this pillar, businesses and organizations can develop cloud-based infrastructures that are efficient, scalable, and financially sustainable over the long term.

The cost optimization pillar of the Microsoft Azure Well-Architected Framework is built on a set of fundamental principles that can help organizations effectively manage their cloud expenses while still achieving optimal performance and scalability:

1. **Adopt a culture of cost awareness and accountability**: Ensure that all stakeholders are aware of the cost implications of their actions and that individuals or teams are held accountable for any unnecessary expenditures. This can be achieved through clear communication, training, and establishing clear guidelines around budgetary constraints.

2. **Monitor and optimize cloud resources continuously**: Regularly review resource usage and identify areas where optimizations can be made to reduce costs without negatively impacting performance. This can include using automation tools to scale resources up or down as needed, identifying idle or underutilized resources and either removing or resizing them, and implementing policies to prevent overprovisioning.

3. **Use cost-effective resources**: Select the most cost-effective resources to meet the needs of your workloads, which can include choosing suitable instance sizes, storage options, and networking configurations. It can also involve using serverless architectures that allow you to pay only for the resources used during a specific execution, reducing costs and eliminating the need to manage infrastructure.

4. **Use reserved instances and savings plans**: Azure offers various types of reservations, which can help reduce long-term resource usage costs. Reserved instances, for example, allow reserving a specific instance type for a one-year or three-year period at a discounted rate. At the same time, savings plans offer similar discounts on usage across a broader range of services. By considering these options, organizations can save thousands of dollars on their cloud expenses each year.

5. **Use cost management and optimization tools**: Azure provides a range of tools and services that can help organizations to monitor, manage, and optimize their cloud expenses. These can include the Microsoft Cost Management + Billing service for Azure, which provides a centralized dashboard for tracking and analyzing costs across all Azure resources. It also offers budget alerts, cost analysis, and recommendations for cost savings based on usage patterns.

You can refer to the following URL to read more about the Azure Well-Architected Framework to optimize costs: `https://bit.ly/az-cost-optimization`

And you can utilize the following tool to evaluate your workload based on the pillars of reliability, cost optimization, operational excellence, security, and performance efficiency: `https://bit.ly/az-well-architected-review`

In the next section, we will review Azure Advisor as a valuable resource for cost optimization in Azure.

Incorporating Azure Advisor best practice recommendations for cost savings

Azure Advisor provides personalized recommendations for optimizing costs based on your specific workloads and usage patterns. These recommendations can help organizations identify areas to reduce expenses without sacrificing performance or functionality.

To access the recommendations provided by Azure Advisor, navigate to the **Cost Management + Billing** blade in the Azure portal, select the **Cost recommendations** option, and then select the **Optimization recommendations** tab.

Figure 6.1: Advisor recommendations

From there, you can view a list of recommendations tailored to your specific environment, including opportunities to reduce costs by resizing or shutting down underutilized resources, identifying and eliminating idle resources, and implementing Azure reservations to save on long-term usage.

In addition to providing recommendations for cost optimization, Microsoft Cost Management + Billing also offers a range of other features and tools to help organizations manage their cloud expenses. This includes cost analysis and budgeting tools, billing and invoice management, and the ability to view usage and cost data across multiple Azure subscriptions and accounts.

Implementing cost management best practices

Effective cost management is crucial for any cloud adoption strategy. As organizations migrate their workloads to the cloud, it becomes imperative for them to efficiently manage their expenses, maximizing the value derived from their cloud investments.

The Microsoft Azure Cloud Adoption Framework provides guidelines and best practices to help organizations manage their cloud expenses and optimize their spending over the long term (`https://learn.microsoft.com/azure/cloud-adoption-framework/`).

One of the key components of the cost management pillar of the Azure Cloud Adoption Framework is developing a comprehensive cost optimization strategy. This involves identifying the key drivers of cloud costs within your organization, developing a set of guidelines and best practices to help manage these costs, and continuously monitoring and optimizing your cloud expenses over time.

The following learning path is recommended to learn more about the Microsoft Azure Well-Architected Framework – Cost optimization learning path: `https://bit.ly/az-cost-optimization-path`

One of the key best practices for cloud cost management is establishing a set of cost management policies and procedures. This involves developing a set of guidelines and best practices for managing cloud expenses within your organization, such as establishing budget limits, monitoring usage patterns, and implementing cost optimization strategies. By establishing clear policies and procedures for managing cloud costs, organizations can ensure that all stakeholders understand their roles and responsibilities and are aligned on cost management goals and objectives.

Another best practice for cloud cost management is to implement automation wherever possible. This can include automating resource provisioning and de-provisioning, implementing autoscaling policies to dynamically adjust resource usage based on demand, or automating cost allocation and chargeback processes to ensure that expenses are accurately allocated to the appropriate business units or cost centers. With automation, organizations can reduce the risk of human error, optimize resource utilization, and save time and effort in managing cloud expenses.

In addition to establishing policies and procedures with automation, organizations should also implement a system for regularly monitoring and analyzing their cloud expenses.

Effective budgeting for Azure services

One of the key challenges organizations face when managing cloud costs is ensuring that they stay within their budgetary constraints. The Microsoft Cost Management + Billing service for Azure provides a range of tools to help organizations manage their cloud expenses effectively, including the ability to set and manage budgets for their Azure services.

To set up a budget in **Cost Management + Billing** for Azure, organizations can use the budget feature, which enables them to define a budget threshold and track their spending against this threshold over time. This can be done at various levels, such as subscription, resource group, or resource level, providing organizations with granular visibility into their cloud expenses and enabling them to identify areas where they may need to adjust their spending patterns.

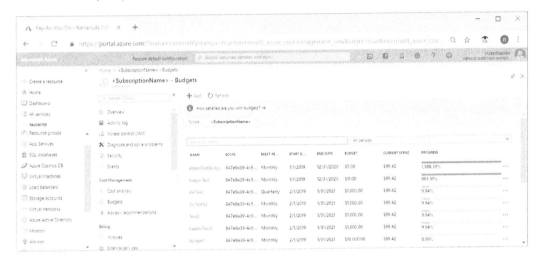

Figure 6.2: Azure Budgets

Once you have established a budget in Azure, you can easily monitor your spending against it to ensure that you stay on track. Azure Budgets provides a simple view of your current spending relative to the defined budget threshold, allowing you to assess whether you need to adjust your cloud spending quickly. Additionally, you can set up alerts to notify you if your spending exceeds a certain percentage of your budget, enabling you to optimize your cloud spending and stay within your financial constraints.

By using Azure Budgets to manage your cloud spending, you can gain greater visibility into your expenses and take proactive steps to optimize your spending over time. Whether you want to control costs, ensure financial sustainability, or optimize your cloud spending for maximum value, Azure Budgets can help you achieve your goals and stay on track with your financial objectives.

We recommend you take a look at the Microsoft Learn module *Introduction to analyzing costs and creating budgets with Microsoft Cost Management:* – `https://bit.ly/az-budgets`

Summary

In this chapter, we discussed the impact of cost optimization in the cloud, which is becoming increasingly important as organizations try to manage their cloud costs and maximize the value of their investments.

We also reviewed how the Microsoft Azure Well-Architected Framework provides guidelines and best practices for developing a cloud-based architecture that is both efficient and cost-effective, with a particular emphasis on the cost optimization pillar. This pillar is based on five fundamental principles: a culture of cost awareness and accountability, continuous monitoring and optimization of cloud resources, using cost-effective resources, considering reserved instances and savings plans, and using cost management and optimization tools.

Conversely, Azure Advisor is a free service that provides personalized recommendations for optimizing Azure resources, including cost savings, based on your usage and performance patterns. Furthermore, Microsoft Cost Management + Billing offers a range of features and tools to help organizations manage their cloud expenses, including cost analysis and budgeting tools, billing and invoice management, and the ability to view usage and cost data across multiple Azure subscriptions and accounts.

Finally, the chapter emphasized the importance of developing a comprehensive cost optimization strategy to manage cloud expenses effectively and optimize spending over the long term.

Next Steps

A strong and well-defined cloud strategy is crucial for organizations to thrive in today's digital landscape. In this book, we explored the core principles of cloud computing and laid the foundation for a comprehensive understanding of Azure's diverse capabilities. By gaining insights into the essence of cloud computing and its evolving models, you can help your organization harness the power of **infrastructure as a service (IaaS)**, **platform as a service (PaaS)**, and **software as a service (SaaS)** – the fundamental building blocks of a cloud strategy. We also explored the concepts of public, private, hybrid, multicloud, and edge computing. Embracing a cloud strategy is essential for organizations aiming to unlock innovation, agility, and scalability while effectively meeting their business objectives.

Chapter 1, Introduction, provided a comprehensive overview of Azure, the different cloud models, and the compelling reasons for choosing Azure as a cloud platform. It provided a solid understanding of the benefits of adopting Azure services, ranging from high availability and scalability to hybrid flexibility and innovative technologies. We highlighted the critical considerations for cloud management, migration, security, and governance, providing valuable insights and best practices. With the guidance provided in this chapter, you can confidently lead your organization through a successful cloud journey.

Chapter 2, Modernizing with Hybrid, Multicloud, and Edge, presented a comprehensive exploration of modernizing with hybrid, multicloud, and edge computing. We emphasized the customer-centric approach and focused on motivations and benefits rather than product-centric discussions. These insights and guidance will help organizations successfully achieve flexibility, scalability, and innovation in their IT infrastructure.

Chapter 3, Migration and Modernization, explored cloud migration, focused on planning and implementation, and detailed best practices for migration and modernization. We provided a range of tools and frameworks to maximize the value of cloud investments and ensure successful migration projects. From workload migration scenarios to achieving cloud scale and performance, you gained practical insights and guidance.

We also covered enterprise-grade backup and disaster recovery strategies to ensure data protection and business continuity. With Azure migration best practices and support, organizations can use the resources, documentation, and training available to guide them through their migration journey. By applying the knowledge and recommendations provided in this chapter, organizations can confidently embrace cloud transformation and unlock the full potential of their IT infrastructure.

Chapter 4, Maximizing Azure Security Benefits for Your Organization, emphasized the importance of identity and access control in maintaining a secure Azure environment. By implementing best practices and implementing the security capabilities of Azure, organizations can fortify their infrastructure and protect against potential threats. Microsoft Sentinel enables intelligent security analytics and threat intelligence, enhancing threat detection and response. We explored various security solutions, such as Microsoft Defender for Cloud, Microsoft Defender for Identity, and Microsoft Defender for Endpoint, enabling organizations to safeguard their cloud resources, endpoints, and sensitive data. Organizations can ensure consistent protection across their entire infrastructure by deploying security solutions from the cloud to the edge. With a focus on securing Kubernetes clusters and ensuring compliance with regulatory requirements, this chapter equipped you with the knowledge and tools to establish a robust and resilient security posture in Azure.

Chapter 5, Automation and Governance in Azure, underscored the reasons for adopting IaC in provisioning Azure infrastructure, such as enhanced speed, consistency, and scalability. We explored the benefits of IaC and showcased the choices available with frameworks such as ARM templates and Bicep. By following best practices and using tools such as Azure DevOps and GitHub, organizations can streamline their IaC workflows and optimize infrastructure deployment. We discussed the comprehensive set of benefits from Azure governance, including control, compliance, and security, facilitated by Azure Blueprints and Azure Policy. We provided the knowledge and tools necessary to harness the power of IaC for efficient and reliable Azure infrastructure provisioning.

Finally, *Chapter 6, Maximizing Efficiency and Cost Savings in Azure*, provided the knowledge and tools to optimize costs in an Azure environment. By using the cost optimization pillar of the Microsoft Azure Well-Architected Framework, organizations can design cloud-based architectures that are efficient and cost-effective. We detailed the best practice recommendations for Azure Advisor to reduce costs and gain actionable insights for eliminating waste and optimizing resource utilization. Implementing cost management governance best practices ensures organizations have the necessary controls to monitor and control costs. We discussed how by creating and managing budgets for Azure services, organizations can utilize their financial budgets in the best possible way. The lessons from this chapter enable organizations to achieve maximum cost efficiency in their Azure deployments while ensuring they extract the most value from their cloud investments.

Index

www.packtpub.com

Subscribe to our online digital library for full access to over 7,000 books and videos, as well as industry leading tools to help you plan your personal development and advance your career. For more information, please visit our website.

Why subscribe?

- Spend less time learning and more time coding with practical eBooks and Videos from over 4,000 industry professionals

- Improve your learning with Skill Plans built especially for you

- Get a free eBook or video every month

- Fully searchable for easy access to vital information

- Copy and paste, print, and bookmark content

Did you know that Packt offers eBook versions of every book published, with PDF and ePub files available? You can upgrade to the eBook version at packtpub.com and as a print book customer, you are entitled to a discount on the eBook copy. Get in touch with us at customercare@packtpub.com for more details.

At www.packtpub.com, you can also read a collection of free technical articles, sign up for a range of free newsletters, and receive exclusive discounts and offers on Packt books and eBooks.

Other Books You May Enjoy

If you enjoyed this book, you may be interested in these other books by Packt:

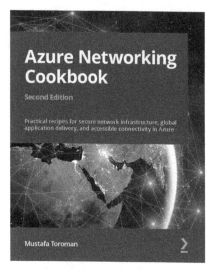

Azure Networking Cookbook - Second Edition

Mustafa Toroman

ISBN: 978-1-80056-375-9

- Learn to create Azure networking services
- Understand how to create and work on hybrid connections
- Configure and manage Azure network services
- Learn ways to design high availability network solutions in Azure
- Discover how to monitor and troubleshoot Azure network resources
- Learn different methods of connecting local networks to Azure virtual networks

Azure Security Cookbook - Second Edition

Steve Miles

ISBN: 978-1-80461-796-0

- Find out how to implement Azure security features and tools
- Understand how to provide actionable insights into security incidents
- Gain confidence in securing Azure resources and operations
- Shorten your time to value for applying learned skills in real-world cases
- Follow best practices and choices based on informed decisions
- Better prepare for Microsoft certification with a security element

Packt is searching for authors like you

If you're interested in becoming an author for Packt, please visit authors.packtpub.com and apply today. We have worked with thousands of developers and tech professionals, just like you, to help them share their insight with the global tech community. You can make a general application, apply for a specific hot topic that we are recruiting an author for, or submit your own idea.

Download a free PDF copy of this book

Thanks for purchasing this book!

Do you like to read on the go but are unable to carry your print books everywhere?

Is your eBook purchase not compatible with the device of your choice?

Don't worry, now with every Packt book you get a DRM-free PDF version of that book at no cost.

Read anywhere, any place, on any device. Search, copy, and paste code from your favorite technical books directly into your application.

The perks don't stop there, you can get exclusive access to discounts, newsletters, and great free content in your inbox daily

Follow these simple steps to get the benefits:

1. Scan the QR code or visit the link below

https://packt.link/free-ebook/9781837639915

2. Submit your proof of purchase
3. That's it! We'll send your free PDF and other benefits to your email directly

Printed in the USA
CPSIA information can be obtained
at www.ICGtesting.com
JSHW060552151223
53706JS00007B/61

9 781837 639915